South Island —
Christ Church — George Hotel
train to W. Coast — near
Glacier — Westwood Lodge

Queenstown area —
    Eichardts Hotel
Glen Orchy — 15 mins
    Blanket Bay Lodge

ESCAPE TO
New Zealand

Photography by Simon Russell
Text by Kirsten Ellis

Fodor's

FODOR'S TRAVEL PUBLICATIONS
NEW YORK • TORONTO • LONDON • SYDNEY • AUCKLAND • WWW.FODORS.COM

First Edition
ISBN 0-676-90882-9

Special Sales
Fodor's Travel Publications are available at special discounts for
bulk purchases for sales promotions or premiums. Special
editions, including personalized covers, excerpts of existing
guides, and corporate imprints, can be created in large
quantities for special needs. For more information, contact your
local bookseller or write to Special Markets, Fodor's Travel
Publications, 280 Park Avenue, New York, NY 10017. Inquiries
from Canada should be directed to your local Canadian
bookseller or sent to Random House of Canada, Ltd., Marketing
Dept., 2775 Matheson Boulevard East, Mississauga, Ontario
L4W 4P7. Inquiries from the United Kingdom should be sent to
Fodor's Travel Publications, 20 Vauxhall Bridge Road, London,
England SW1V 2SA.

Acknowledgments
From Simon Russell: Thanks to Kirsten for her energy and humor
through all our adventures. To Simone, Jayne, and Kirstie of
Tourism New Zealand and to Steve at Qantas for flying us in
luxury—thanks so much, we couldn't have done it without you.
Thanks to Liane and Richard for the best ride on the high seas;
to Molly and Kai for making me feel like family; to Beth and Te
Warena for your invaluable insights into the Maori spirit. As
always, hats off to the Escape team. But most of all a big kiss
and hug to Ann and Aidan.

From Kirsten Ellis: Thanks to Simon, who made working on this
book a fun adventure; to Fabrizio La Rocca, for his stylish vision;
and to Chris Swiac, for her insight. Thanks to Tom, my husband,
for all his support; to my parents, Louise Longdin and Howard
Ellis, for not dissuading me from exploring the world at an early
age; and to Jules Longdin-Prisk and Ian, Nik, and Tom Eagles.
Special thanks to Michael Carlson, Lesley Downer, and Zillah
Bosworth-Coleman. I owe a particular gratitude to Pamela Windo;
Steve Kernaghan at Qantas; Simone Flight, Kirstie Bedford and
Jayne Marshall of Tourism New Zealand; Molly Schwarz and Kai
Hawkins; Beth Coleman; and Carmel Hotai Cochrane.

Credits
Creative Director and Series Editor: Fabrizio La Rocca
Editorial Director: Karen Cure
Art Director: Tigist Getachew

Editor: Christine Swiac
Editorial Assistant: Dennis Sarlo
Editorial Production: Taryn Luciani
Production/Manufacturing: C. R. Bloodgood, Robert B. Shields
Maps: David Lindroth, Inc.

Other Escape Guides
Escape to the Amalfi Coast • Escape to the American Desert
Escape to the Wine Country • Escape to Ireland
Escape to Morocco • Escape to Northern New England •
Escape to Provence • Escape to the Riviera • Escape to Tuscany
Available in bookstores

Most books on the travel shelves are either long on the nitty-gritty and short on evocative photographs, or the other way around. We at Fodor's think that the different balance in this slim volume is just perfect, rather like the intersection of the most luscious magazine article and a sensible, down-to-earth guidebook. On the road, the useful pages at the end of the book are practically all you need. For the planning, roam through the photographs up front: Each reveals a key facet of New Zealand and, taken with the lyrical accompanying text, conveys a sense of place that will take you there before you go. Each page opens up an exceptional New Zealand experience; each spread leads you to the quintessential places that highlight the spirit of this country at its purest.

Some of these places are sure to beckon. You may yearn for solitary walks in lichen-shrouded rain forests or horseback rides through tussock-cloaked hills on the fringes of the Southern Alps. You may dream of a fireplace-warmed cabin on a rocky, windswept beach or picture a glacial landscape of blue-tinged ice grottos and pitted snowy pinnacles. Sip kava at a festival celebrating Pacific Island cultures, or pinot noir amid vineyards and orchards. Explore the waters, from sea to sound to stream, in a ketch or a kayak. Or curl up by the window in a lakeside lodge. Whatever your pleasure, give yourself the chance to remember what it's like to follow the open road.

To capture the magic of New Zealand, American photographer Simon Russell and author Kirsten Ellis, herself New Zealand–born, navigated slippery caves, rowed through foggy fjords, maneuvered around sheep gridlock, and traipsed through fern-filled forests. Never one to turn down a challenge, Russell bungee-jumped from a bridge and climbed masts to get the right shots of this action-oriented country. "At first it was the incredible drama of the New Zealand landscape that drew me," he said. "But the longer I stayed, the more I realized that the spirit and energy of the people are just as captivating."

Follow in their footsteps. Forget your projects and deadlines, and escape to New Zealand. You owe it to yourself.

—The Editors

ON YOUR FIRST MORNING, YOU WAKE TO THE ROAR OF BOOMING SURF, wondering how you slept so soundly. Sunlight beams through the stained-glass windows, flooding the bedspread with their colors. Sleepily you pad about the secluded wooden cottage, cradling a warm mug, before throwing wide the doors onto the sun-splashed veranda and stepping out. Glimmering through Dr. Seuss–style cabbage trees and feathery *toi toi* and russet *maram* grasses is that hypnotic silvery line where the Tasman Sea merges with the sky. Is this how it would be to stand on the very edge of the world? For now you are sole witness to the magnificent drama of the coal-black dunes, crashing breakers, gnarled rocks, and forested headlands—and the mysterious, drifting mists that drape them all. *Caw! Caw!* Even the seagulls seem

Beach of Black Sand *&* Mist

A COTTAGE STAY ON AUCKLAND'S WILD WEST COAST

Fairy folk cavort on Bethells Beach— or so you may sense as you gaze out over its soulful black sands from your private cottage high above the Tasman Sea.

reverent here as they wheel higher among giant temples of clouds. A mood of wild exuberance lifts you, too, and you scamper to the shoreline. The wind ruffles your hair and froth laps at your ankles. Here and there large kelp strands reminiscent of strange South Pacific sea monsters quiver slightly, and whorl-like shells appear like tiny question marks studding the sand. Back at the cottage, a wide-brim hat, a homemade cake, and a set of watercolor paints await. You pack a picnic lunch. When the day warms up, you set off on a streamside trail to Lake Wainamu, where you leap down billowy dunes into the freshwater depths. On the walk back, the whir of wood pigeons punctuates the hush of the surrounding emerald bush, which is dotted with clusters of blood-red pohutakawa blossoms. Tonight, you think, you'll grill up something simple, maybe tossing in some rosemary from the garden, and dine under the stars of the southern hemisphere.

Cottage for rent: stained-glass windows, kitchen with view, nothing but maram grass all around. Karekare Beach, filmed in *The Piano*, is down the road.

Saddle up and go for a gallop down
the strand before lunch, swim in
a freshwater lake, or venture into
the emerald bush of the Waitakere
Ranges. You may feel as if no one
else is around, yet Auckland is just
45 minutes away.

"For a *falangi* like you, ten dollars, mate." At the one-day Pasifika Festival, you hear a medley of languages, from Nuiean to Samoan, and English with every conceivable Polynesian accent. Highly rhythmic drumming pulsates in the background, and you can almost taste the frangipani, coconut oil, and steamed taro on the breeze. You weave your way through the mélange: plump Tokelaun girls wearing flowery wreaths on their knee-length hair; sweet-faced Cook Island matrons in identical muumuu-style frocks; cinnamon-skinned boys in Hawaiian shirts; and bare-chested Tongan men with tree-trunk thighs swathed in woven skirts. The stalls offer everything from raffia hula skirts to Jonah Lomu T-shirts — well, the rugby star is of Tongan descent. Under one tarp, Samoan

Woven Strands of Polynesia

THE PASIFIKA FESTIVAL, AUCKLAND

In case you should overlook it, the sights and sounds of Pasifika will remind you: Auckland is unquestionably the capital of the South Pacific.

tatau artist Peter Suluape demonstrates the ancient method of *a'au* tattooing, his willing victim wincing as finishing touches are made to the design. Under another, large Tongan ladies, hair pulled back in tight buns, show how they strip mulberry bark, pound it into tapa cloth, and stain it with delicate, geometric motifs. You pull out your wallet when you come to a treasure trove of *tivaevae,* the Cook Island quilts stitched with bright patterns taken from nature: flame vines, coconut palms, lilies, red ginger stems. Purchase in hand, you're ready to eat. Carefully considering the made-for-the-masses delicacies, you make your picks: sweet liquid poured from a coconut hacked open with a machete and fish wrapped in banana leaves and steamed over hot stones. Gingerly, you try a glass of *kava,* the milky, soporific potion made from the ground roots of pepper plants. Suddenly, the drumming intensifies and a line of Cook Island women shimmies into view, as sultry as the March afternoon, hips furiously shaking. The crowd roars in approval.

Support our local homegrown music....
SAMOA ROCKS!!!
TALOFA!!!
I love it because it's much warmer than Scotland and the men are better looking! Claire
Great day
Great weather
Great idea
The Pacific's a cool place to be! Tim-10
SOUTHSIDE
GREAT PEOPLE,
OF AROHA.
PASIFICA IS
MARAMA
GOD BLESS YOU
A FANTASTIC PLACE WITH FANTASTIC PEOPLE.
AUCKLAND IS THE
Because people unite and have their
individuality!!

Threads of life from the kaleidoscope of islands beyond New Zealand's shores are woven into the fabric of the city as tightly as a well-strung lei; at the one-day festival, cultural "villages" highlight the different textures of the islands.

BEDROOM, LIVING ROOM, BATHROOM. EVERY ROOM OF YOUR COTTAGE at Matakauri Lodge has the view, a breathtaking, unobstructed panorama of glass-smooth Lake Wakatipu and the craggy snow-flecked mountains that frame it. From your private patio you take in the cluster of low wood-and-stone buildings—they seem to have taken a cue from the Prairie School—and the native bush that surrounds them. Dead ahead the Cecil and Walter peaks loom large, just on the other side of the sapphire waters above which you seem to float, and the Remarkables stretch to your left. No signs that Queenstown is less than 10 miles away, and no crowds; the lodge includes only four cottages and three suites in the main building. With supersize skylights and walls of windows, the main lounge invites further contemplative gazing. Native-beech trim,

Lakeside Lair

MATAKAURI LODGE, QUEENSTOWN

After a brisk walk on the pebbly beach, you can continue your contemplation of Lake Wakatipu, the country's longest lake, in soapy serenity.

cushy upholstery, richly patterned wool rugs, and colorful pieces by New Zealand artists take the edge off the cool slate and stone. You try out all the vantage points, pausing at each to soak up the scenery. After an afternoon walk on the private fringe of beach beneath the lodge, you retreat with a book to an outdoor chair at your cottage. But try as you might to focus on the text, it can't compete with the landscape. Your oversize bathtub, under an oversize window, is perfect for watching the setting sun turn lake and sky first pink, then orange, scarlet, and finally, dusky lavender. Reluctantly, you pull yourself away; dinner awaits, served tonight in the candlelit wine cellar. Sushi hors d'oeuvres and a swallow of a local chardonnay re-energize you, but after the meal you're just as happy to be back in your cottage, on the couch in front of the fire with a glass of port, knowing you'll wake tomorrow to that view.

Why go anywhere
else on the South
Island? Matakauri
Lodge makes the
hustle and bustle
of Queenstown feel
very far away.

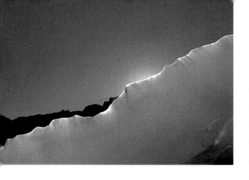

IT BEGINS WITH THE DEAFENING WHIR OF THE HELICOPTER, A BENT-OVER dash across the tarmac in your hobnailed boots, the clamber up into the red bubble. Your stomach lurches as you take off and whirl up to an eagle's view over rain forests, waterfalls, and, then, nothing but rocks. On to Fox Glacier, New Zealand's most spectacular icefall, a towering, choppy tongue of ice that licks the sides of cleft mountains. In no time, it seems, you and your small group of companions for the next few hours are deposited, though not quite marooned. Excited but anxious, you lace up your crampons, following the guide's instructions, and learn to stabilize yourself with your ice poles. At first you teeter cautiously forward like some steel-clad stork, awed by the frozen beauty all around, placing one deliberate step after the other until a sort of

Catacombs of Ice

A GUIDED WALK ON FOX GLACIER, WESTLAND NATIONAL PARK

A mighty river of ice edges between the 10,000-foot peaks of South Island's Westland National Park at a rate of up to 3 feet a day, flowing downhill almost to the sea.

bravado sets in—the only choice is to go on. Under the azure sky and the blinding, supercharged light, you find yourself navigating blue-tinged ice caves, cascading whipped-cream pinnacles, and crevasses so precipitous that your heart thuds. All the while, the sounds of melting echo unseen beneath your feet. *Crunch, crunch, splish, splash.* The groan and creak of ice are not unlike the gentle, relentless heaving of a sailboat. Just as the ethereal nature of the landscape starts to sink in, you hear a more ominous crack and shudder at the prospect of a sudden, sliding skid. At that moment Colin, your bearded guide, holds out his strong, tanned hand. Some of your companions, however, have managed to charge ahead with the ease and élan of mountain goats. Soon enough you're back where you started, elated to be in one piece, your mind dazzled by the intricate palette of ice, the kaleidoscope beneath the cloak of white. Still, you're grateful to hear the helicopter returning to pluck you away.

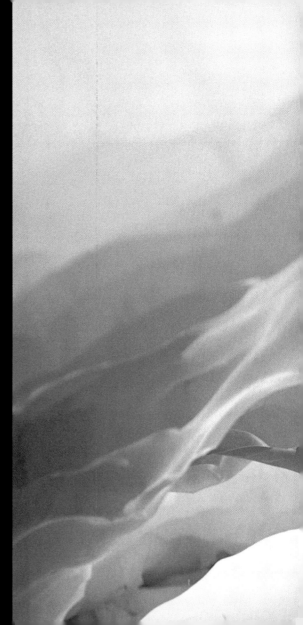

A helicopter whisks you over
verdant rain forest before
landing on the stable névé of
Fox Glacier, a blue–white world
of caves and pinnacles that's
difficult to reach otherwise.

The Realm of the Tuhoe

TE UREWERA NATIONAL PARK

YOU MAY INTUIT SOMETHING MYSTERIOUS IN THE VIRGIN FORESTS OF TE UREWERA NATIONAL PARK, a certain sense of the sacred. Even the drive to the park, hours along dusty Highway 38 without seeing a soul, reminds you that this is a world apart. The road climbs into the mountains, its serpentine twists leading you through timber-lined chasms, past reverberating waterfalls, and deep into the wilderness. Tremendous trees swathed in ghostly drifts of lichen tower all about like guardians of a secretive, brooding, primeval world. This is the land of the Tuhoe, the Maori tribe members who call themselves the "Children of the Mist"; their ancestors, so the legend goes, were born of supernatural beings, sprung from the mountains and the white fog surrounding them. Proud and independent, the Tuhoe have had their own prophets, their own language, their own vision of a blood connection to the land. You can see this fierce independence in their faces—and sometimes in their silence as visitors enter their realm. But you come here lightly, only for a few days, to explore the forest's hidden treasures.

By nightfall you are tucked away in a homey wooden cabin on the lapped foreshore of Lake Waikaremoana, ready for sleep. But for the mournful cry of the morepork, the country's native owl, the night is still; no sign of the *taniwha*, the mythical water monster said to live here. When the morning sun has etched the lake's surface with silver ripples, you clamber aboard a stalwart water taxi with Noel, the gruffly humorous, if somewhat taciturn, Tuhoe skipper, and rocket across choppy waters to walk the farthermost shores. The lakeside circuit usually takes four days, but even a few hours are enough to savor the intense solitude. Nothing here seems to have changed since writer Katharine Mansfield noted in the early 1900s: "It is all so gigantic and tragic—and even in the high sunlight it is so passionately secret."

Forget creature comforts: Lose yourself in this ancient tract of forest, a world of eerie stillness— for a few hours or a few days.

THE FERRY RIDE FROM AUCKLAND TAKES JUST OVER 30 MINUTES, BUT Longhouse, a hilltop hideaway on Waiheke Island, seems a world away from the lights now twinkling over distant Waitemata Harbour. Olive groves, vineyards, and an organic garden surround the cliff-hugging house, a cooking school and retreat that is also home to Molly Schwarz and Kai Hawkins. There's an improvised quality to staying here—whether you're learning to bake bread in the handsome open-air wood-fired oven, picking your way along headland paths to beaches fringed by flowery pohutukawa trees, exploring trails around the island's less-populated coves on a rented moped, visiting one of Waiheke's outstanding wine makers, or taking a siesta on a canopy bed, lulled by the chirping of cicadas. "We had this vision of living by the sea for a long time,

Island Aerie

STAYING AT LONGHOUSE, WAIHEKE ISLAND

Longhouse embodies the essence of Waiheke, an island discovered by potters and alternative life-stylers that remains mellow and bohemian to this day.

a place where learning about food and sharing ideas could be sociable and inspiring, an extension of the way we've always lived, really," explains Molly, a self-described decorator, entrepreneur, and lover of unusual objects and all things Mexican. It's that vision that draws a rotating cast of respected chefs to Longhouse from New Zealand and abroad, to offer master classes that can span several days or a week. Tonight you happily join the makings of an impromptu dinner party in the spare and lofty kitchen. Paul, one of Molly's adult children and a talented chef himself, whisks a red-curry marinade for a huge snapper caught a few hours earlier, then glazes racks of milk-fed lamb with a rosemary-perfumed mushroom reduction, and puts the final touches on a cake of frangipane and puff pastry. In the dining room, candles flicker on the big oak table as the waves murmur on the black sea below. "Come and eat, everyone," Molly calls. Who could resist?

Is that the bossa nova throbbing faintly down the hall? Did you just catch the clink of ice in a cocktail shaker? Bread's in the oven and someone's shucking oysters. Outside, a living canvas of islands, blue bay, and shifting clouds unfurls with the same unhurried pace.

REMOTE AND OTHERWORLDLY, FIORDLAND NATIONAL PARK HAS TWO guises, one glimpsed from water and the other from land. But it's from the water that you can begin to comprehend the breadth and the scale of this vast wilderness—the 3 million acres of mountains, fjords, lakes, forests, river valleys, and isolated coast that make up New Zealand's largest national park. And it is water, in all its forms, that rules this elusive landscape—mist and cloud, stream and lake, snow and ice, and, especially, rain. Lucky for you, the morning has brought silvery light and cloudscape drama instead of showers. Gauzy layers of fog enfold the distant expanses of ancient rain forest and the jagged, frosted peaks surrounding Milford Sound; the gentle air-kisses of mist that land on your skin and hair are a refreshing change from the strong

Into the Sound

FIORDLAND NATIONAL PARK

One of the world's wettest places, Milford Sound gets about 240 inches of precipitation each year, but even downpours don't dampen its beauty.

sun that reigns most everywhere else in this country. For now, only the glide of the kayak and the dip of your paddle interrupt the icy stillness, which can appear as brilliant as the region's prized greenstone one moment and as inky as the black coral formations lying deep beneath the surface the next. In every direction, spectacular scenery vies for your attention; the sight of a bottlenose dolphin, a crested penguin, or some rare black butterflies would be an added bonus. The soundtrack to all this is the gurgle of water from the countless hidden falls, hundreds of them cascading down the sheer granite cliffs from high glacial mountain pools and lakes. Some move in trickles, while others, such as 1,900-foot Sutherland Falls—it can be seen along that most famous of New Zealand's walks, the Milford Track—charge down in torrents, their pounding energy fueling the constant spray of dewy particles that feeds Fiordland's luminous lichen, ferns, and acid-green moss.

Waterfalls wash over sheer
walls of rock that rise right
from the sounds, bays,
and inlets and are cloaked
with luxuriant rain forest.

Glacier-carved valleys, massed wildflowers, gushing falls, flora-rich woods: Almost every step along the famed Milford Track, a four-day bush walk, offers awe-inspiring views in all the shades of green and blue.

"FOR US MAORI, IF YOU GET TOO FAR AWAY FROM YOUR *WAIRUA*— your spirit—you lose your connection to the land, the spiritual blueprint you were born with, the breath of creation that formed you," says Carmel Hotai Cochrane, a gifted spiritual healer from the Nga Phui *iwi* (tribe). In her Auckland studio you close your eyes and entrust this gentle woman with body and spirit. To shift negative energies—jet lag, perhaps, or anxiety over a long journey home—she moves her hands above and around you, emitting extraordinary wind-like breathing sounds, an age-old technique called *te hau mariri*. "Many of our words have a sacred meaning; our ancient people meant them to have an empowering quality," she explains. Even the everyday greeting *kia ora*, she adds, has another meaning: "I empower you with the life force of the divine

The Sacred Breath

A MAORI RENAISSANCE

Intricate patterns, on flesh and wood, speak of ancestral journeys, ancient gods, and veneration for the land and the power of nature.

energy." And so it is that you experience the resurgence of the Maori language, a revival which itself is part of a larger renaissance, a movement referred to as Maoritanga, celebrating Maori culture and tradition. With the blessing of their elders, many young Maori wear *ta moko*, or tattoos—especially on their thighs and buttocks, like traditional warriors—and speak with pride about their people's oral traditions. Everywhere you go on the islands you see symbols from the Maori domain, from the unfurling *koru* (fern frond), which signifies rebirth and serves as the tail logo for the national air carrier, to the treasured greenstone, or jade, which is fashioned into amulets. As the country strives to move into the future without forgetting its history, the Maori face their own challenge, to avoid straying too far from their *wairua*. But they are confident they will succeed. "Going into the future with our culture strong, to be peaceful warriors, this may be our greatest strength," Carmel says.

The Lure of the Trout

FLY-FISHING THE TONGARIRO-TAUPO RIVER

YOU WEREN'T GOING TO MISS A CHANCE TO FISH THE FAMED WATERS OF THE TAUPO REGION WITH a modern master of the trout-fishing world. From the moment Greg Catley whisked you through seemingly impenetrable bush in his mud-splattered jeep, helped you suit up, and led you across shale- and boulder-bottomed streams to some of his favorite spots, you knew you were in good hands. Now it's midmorning, and you're trying to at least keep your balance in green waders, thigh deep in the swift and icy Tongariro-Taupo River. Katie Bean, Greg's dutiful English springer, trots across the marshes, apparently aware that she mustn't bark and scare away the fish. Otherwise, only the sounds of darting swallows and bellbirds and the swirling plish-plash of the water break the stillness. *Fsssshoowwww!* Greg casts into the glinting waters with a single flick of his wrist. In an instant he reels in a huge, wriggly rainbow trout, all speckled and roseate. But just as you're mentally preparing dinner, he releases it unscathed. "Too small," he says.

Not a fly fisherman in New Zealand speaks of the winter spawning runs into the Lake Taupo tributary streams with anything less than reverence.

"We get ten-pounders here." From the rugged-Kiwi-outdoorsman school of ribald straight talk, Greg has fished the area's streams and lakes practically all his life and usually throws back his catches. The sudden tugging on your rod no longer makes your heart stop, but that's because you know the real challenge is the struggle that follows. "That's it, Tiger, play the fish," Greg coaches. "You've gotta give it a good hard yank." Here is your reminder that reeling them in is truly an art—and an elusive one at that. After a break to rest your arms and reconsider your technique over lunch, you return to your casting even more determined to dine on trout tonight. Alas, it is not to be. Instead, it's off for a hot bath and fresh clothes. You'll be back tomorrow.

IN THE HIGH SOLITARY PLATEAU SHADOWED BY MOUNT MISERY AND Mount Horrible is the Valley of the Rainbows, or Te Ko Awa o Aniwaniwa, of Maori legend. The elements can be harsh among these snow-dusted alpine peaks, which tower over green pastureland where sheep outnumber humans 4,000 to one. Yet when clouds lift after torrential rains to reveal multicolored double arcs, the valley shimmers. Amid this rugged beauty is the Grasmere Lodge. Part of a working farm that keeps sheep, cattle, and deer, it's as luxurious a refuge as can be imagined in this setting. Once one of the largest high-country sheep ranches in New Zealand, the property has been whittled to 1,500 acres from its original 43,000—some of the land absorbed by the surrounding Arthur's Pass National Park. But the sense of isolation hasn't diminished

Up at the Farm

A STAY AT GRASMERE LODGE, CASS

In this epic big-sky landscape, vast verdured plateaus stretch to monumental peaks and man and beast are reduced to mere specks.

over the years. You arrive via a long, narrow highway from Christchurch that climbs through awesome chasms, or by the TranzAlpine Express, from which you alight at a lonesome railway crossing where a Range Rover awaits to take you a bit farther still. You can muck about with the animals here, try your hand at sheep-shearing or some of the other farming activities, or saddle up to explore the trails that vein the tussock-covered hillsides. Entire days can be spent fishing with a guide by your side. Or you may prefer to soak up all that fresh air and silence without bothering to leave your teak chaise by the heated pool. In the pause before a four-course meal at an elegant mahogany table set with candles, you can warm up with a drink in front of the fire. Settled into a leather couch, you may hear about the difficult conditions encountered by the early settlers— swagmen and greenstone-toting Maori. As beautiful as they are, Mount Misery and Mount Horrible got their names for a reason.

Stillness is the province of this mountain realm, broken only by the soft roll of the clouds, the expanses of whispering tussock, and the crackling of the poolside fire.

IN A CREAM LINEN SUIT, GREEN-AND-WHITE-STRIPED TIE, MATCHING boater, and clipped mustache, Wesley Golledge is a vision of the complete Edwardian gentleman, cycling to the boat shed on an antique penny farthing. "Our heritage is English," the Christchurch resident explains proudly. "We got away from being part of the Mother Country, but our Englishness still defines us." Built in 1882, the Antigua Boatshed today is a shrine to England, circa 1936. Inside, vintage boys' blazers in traditional school colors, old bottles—some with sprigs of flowers, one bearing the Union Jack—and framed illustrations from Boys' Own annuals line the walls; a quotation from Kenneth Grahame, author of *The Wind in the Willows*, hangs above the door. Outside, bobbing on the Avon River, are the *Albert*, *Victoria*, and *Queen Elizabeth II*, which were modeled on

An Edwardian River Glide

PUNTING ON THE AVON, CHRISTCHURCH

Icons of the Empire are everywhere in this South Island city, garden-obsessed and perpetually abloom. Punt under the dappled shade of a sunny afternoon, or go by moonlight, sipping mulled wine.

classic Cambridge punts. Before you head down the river, Wesley offers a blazer or blanket. How about musical accompaniment? Champagne? And you mustn't forget the brown paper bag of bread for the ducks—"Someone's always got to be feeding the ducks." As Wesley propels the punt along the Avon, you glimpse the city's Victorian-era Gothic buildings, and the occasional restored vintage electric tram, which rattles peaceably by. The transparent, spring-fed river winds through the heart of Christchurch and its Botanic Gardens, where brilliantly pink azaleas scatter their petals like confetti. Alas, it's too late to witness the spectacle of the 650,000 daffodils that carpet the riverbanks each September. But how enjoyable it is to slow to such a gentle pace and to watch the swallows and the exquisite dragonflies darting about, and the speckled ducklings bobbing for breadcrumbs. Already it's time to get back—too soon, it seems— and the dreamy interlude is over. Now would be the perfect time for a Devonshire tea.

Restored antique trams, stained-glass windows, Victorian gothic architecture, the Christchurch Cathedral, and the carefully tended Botanic Gardens set the tone in Christchurch. Britannia still rules.

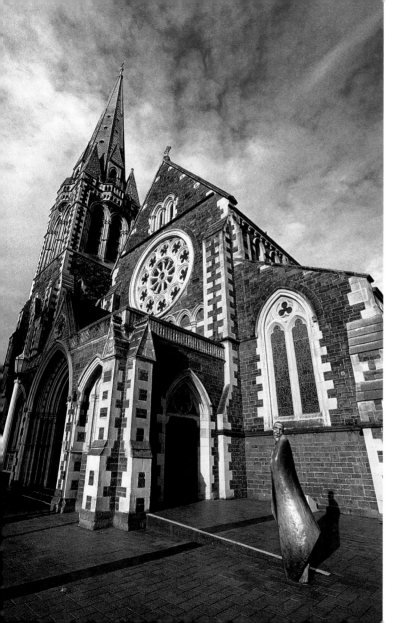

ESCAPE TO NEW ZEALAND

WHO COULD RESIST PARADISE? THE TINY COLONIAL-ERA SETTLEMENT about 40 miles from Queenstown is surrounded by the lichen-and-moss-filled forests that served as a magical backdrop for parts of *The Lord of the Rings*. But storybook scenery is nearly everywhere you go around Queenstown, and seeing it astride a horse somehow makes you part of it. Your journey starts in Glenorchy, a rustic hamlet at the north tip of serene Lake Wakatipu, a few minutes by car from your lodgings at Blanket Bay. How fitting that Tabasco, your chocolate-colored steed for the day, was an armor-clad extra in the cinematic take on the Tolkien tale. Today your merry band includes a couple of English newlyweds and an accountant from Hong Kong; leading you is Charley, a tan South Islander in oilskin chaps who has a no-nonsense-farmer's-daughter way about

Riding the High Country

TAKING TO THE SADDLE IN GLENORCHY

In the saddle, you experience the sensation of being nearer the heavens and yet more in tune with the movements of the earth under hooves.

her but knows when to dispense a reassuring smile. Single file under the clear November sky, you meander along the Rees River, its willow-lined banks woven through with a rainbow of spiky wildflowers. In the distance ahead, the snowy ridges of Mount Aspiring National Park seem to rise right from the water. Tabasco picks his way across sand beds and shale, sometimes splashing in the milky turquoise shallows. Up to his flanks in the deeper sections, he strains against the fast-flowing current as you bring your legs up higher, hoping for no unplanned swims. But the horse remains surefooted, his hooves steady on the slick rocks. Where the landscape broadens into grassy high-country fields fringed with poplar and weather-bleached fences, you're free to stride at your own pace, maybe break into a trot, canter, or gallop. Within a few hours, you return, saddle-sore but exhilarated, from Middle-Earth. Or was it Paradise?

Several worlds seem to merge along the ridged spine that runs most of the length of the South Island: cragged, white peaks loom over broad swaths of grassland and ribbons of aqua waters.

IF EVER THERE WERE A PLACE TO GET IN TOUCH WITH YOUR INNER ARNOLD (AS IN Schwarzenegger, a well-regarded visitor in these parts), this is it. So what if your Arnold seems to be in hiding as you perch at the edge of the platform, bungee fastened, knees bent, torso forward, eyes fixed on the swirling waters 150 feet below. For one heart-stopping instant you manage to push past the fear, and— *aaaaaaaaahhh*—down you go, plummeting in a head-first free fall toward the Kawarau River. It's a quick trip, over in a few seconds. "Doesn't it just blow your mind?" a fellow jumper asks breathlessly as you clamber up the thyme-sprigged hillside after the drop. Your heart is pumping hard, your head is reeling, and your ears are throbbing with that energy surge triggered by the shock to your system. What is it that moves normally phlegmatic souls to exchange rational thought for a rush of adrenaline—to leap into

A Shot of Adrenaline

ADVENTURING FORTH IN QUEENSTOWN

Fasten your seatbelt: Chockablock with adventure outfitters, Queenstown is the perfect place for a joyride or two.

ravines, soar from the hillsides harnessed to billowy sails, jet boat through rocky gorges, or even rocket across the sky strapped to a James Bond–style contraption? Around Queenstown such diversions are plentiful, inspired in part by the superlative natural setting of towering ocher-flanked mountains and steep chasms, emerald-blue rivers, and satin-surfaced, glacier-fed lakes. In addition to the desire to get closer to nature, there's Queenstown's indomitable spirit, a kind of homage to the early gold-hungry pioneers who managed the impossible: carving a road through nearby Skipper's Canyon and over some of the world's most treacherous mountain passes. This infectious "anything is possible" mentality grabs hold of you. Next stop: the Shotover Jet, a high-speed fire engine–red boat that hurtles over rapids, flirting with sheer cliff walls, and pirouettes—yes, in full turns—across the waves. "Don't forget to hold on, folks," the driver yells as the beast revs up. Indeed.

MAYBE IT WAS THE SIGHT OF ALL THOSE SLEEK ÜBER-YACHTS AND the flotilla of muscular catamarans lined up along Auckland's café-thronged Viaduct Basin, or perhaps it was just the carefree way everyone here takes to the water whenever the sun shines: you had to join them. So here you are, basking on the deck of the classically restored 72-foot ketch *Ranui*, all gleaming brass and warm wood, her four sails billowing with the 12-knot breeze, ready to cast off for a night at sea. "Stand about!" Skipper Richard Allen—a former Olympic sailor with a wide, boyish smile—invites you to steer. The boat curls gracefully through the foam-capped waves and rounds the giant slumbering volcanic island of Rangitoto, the icon that dominates the city's seascape. Beyond lie other secluded islands, some bucolic with sheep-dotted rolling farmland speckled with brightly

A Sail Set into the Blue

CRUISING THE ISLANDS OF THE HAURAKI GULF

Contemplate the graceful fusion of sea, sky, and land, from aboard the Ranui ("bright sun" in Maori), a 1936 ketch that's all polished native kauri, totara, and Malaysian teak.

painted houses, others preserved wild and empty as nature made them. Liane Farry, Richard's partner and a former restaurateur, offers you a glass of sauvignon blanc as the tantalizing aromas emerging from the galley announce lunch. In no time you are moored off one of Rakino's tiny white-sand bays, skin tingling from a salty plunge. Where next? You survey the outlines of the Hauraki Gulf islands on a map: Motutapu, Waiheke, Kawau. The rest of the world has receded, reduced to a sliver. As sunset brushes vivid feathers across pearly clouds, an inflatable dinghy transports you to a sheltered beach where you can pull deliciously briny oysters off the rock and shuck them on the spot. After a hot shower in your cabin, you're ready for serious cocktails, a seafood feast, and some comfortable banter around the table. At the end of the day, take a moment on deck to bid the rising moon good-night before you retire to your bed below, to sleep cocooned, distantly aware of the creak of planks and canvas, letting the sea air work its magic.

Anchoring in secluded bays, rocky coves, and even sea caves, you can sail for a few hours, a few days, or longer, in the Hauraki Gulf, off the Auckland shore. Or chase the horizon farther up the North Island, toward the aptly named Bay of Islands.

AT DAWN WHEN YOU STARTED OUT FOR TONGARIRO NATIONAL PARK, YOU COULDN'T quite imagine how dramatic a hike amid active volcanoes could be. Even now, trekking across the scorched, Mars-like terrain surrounded by snowy slopes and twisted layers of lava, the scenery is too surreal to digest. As you trudge up the steep scoria- and pumice-covered saddle between the Tongariro and Ngauruhoe mountains, the wind seems intent on snatching your clothes, your breath, your soul. "Now you know why it's called the Devil's Staircase," shouts Shane Orchard, rugged and ruddy-faced, your guide on the 10-mile trail called the Tongariro Crossing. Hour after hour you climb, legs aching, to reach the apex of the trail at Red Crater. Peer into the giant, orange-tinged cleft; walk to the edge of its cavernous lip if you dare. Skeins of flickering red lava send up smoke while the heat of the volcanic soil makes its way through your boots.

Among the Volcanoes

HIKING TONGARIRO CROSSING, TONGARIRO NATIONAL PARK

Reminders of the earth's latent fury, snow-capped Tongariro, Ngauruhoe, and Ruapehu dominate this North Island preserve, sacred Maori lands donated to the New Zealand people in 1887. A hushed peace reigns.

Gingerly you begin your descent from this unnatural crest, careful not to tumble, the smell of sulfur in your nostrils. Neither bird nor tree rises from the harsh, eerie landscape, but there, before you, is an exquisite sight: the brilliant Blue and Emerald lakes. Under the high, strong sun, you pause for a picnic lunch, Mount Ruapehu in direct view; the tallest and most lively of the park's volcanoes—and the Mount Doom of *The Lord of the Rings* movie—it last exploded in 1996, spewing fiery boulders into the air. Better not to think about whether a stray footstep could trigger such an outburst. The comforting colors of the land return as the track makes its way through high tussocks covered with lichen and tiny alpine flowers and past the mud pools and furiously spraying fumaroles of Ketetahi Springs. Your legs adjust to the descent and, soon, exhausted but exhilarated, you are welcomed back to Earth by the mountain beech groves at trail's end.

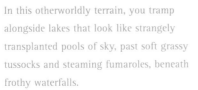

In this otherworldly terrain, you tramp
alongside lakes that look like strangely
transplanted pools of sky, past soft grassy
tussocks and steaming fumaroles, beneath
frothy waterfalls.

IT'S FESTIVAL DAY IN TINY, COLONIAL-ERA MARTINBOROUGH, AND your "ticket" is a wine glass you wear on a ribbon around your neck. Matrons in linen and pumps, food-lovers clad in black, young couples with matching tans, a smattering of executives and politicians—most of Wellington seems to be here this spring morning, wine and revelry in mind. Once a sleepy dairy-farming backwater, the Wairarapa Valley, just over the hills from the capital, is home to a thriving community of boutique vineyards, and its vibrant wines have been raising eyebrows among cognoscenti. Before any imbibing, there's time for an improvised breakfast at the local wine center, a renovated garage that doubles as informal town hall—albeit one where you can buy 200 varieties of pinot noir, as well as artisanal cheeses, organic fruit, flaky-fresh pastries, assorted charcuterie, and old-

Toast Martinborough

A FESTIVAL OF FOOD, WINE, AND MUSIC IN WAIRARAPA

Braided rows of vines crisscross the gentle hills on the south end of the North Island. A bevy of festivals celebrates their bounty.

fashioned jams. Cars aren't allowed at this fete of food, wine, and music, but most of the wineries on your map are within easy walking distance, and you can always climb aboard a weathered vintage bus or a horse-drawn carriage. An energetic jazz band is in full swing at Te Kairanga vineyard, where gardens of roses and jasmine invite loungers to linger. Through the music you catch strains of someone debating the finer points of the newly released sauvignon blanc: "Can you taste the capsicum, or is it more like passion fruit?" At the Ata Rangi vineyard, the stage is set for a barn dance, with large white tents, waiters in aprons and boaters, artfully arranged haystacks and barrels, and clusters of seats. The sizzle and smell of sausages is irresistible; everyone's jostling for some. Ah, but the whitebait fritters are the perfect match for that buttery chardonnay. The band's bluesy ballads beckon the crowd to dance, and the mood mellows along with the late-afternoon sun.

A SMALL BEACH-FRINGED CITY ON TASMAN BAY, NELSON IS ONE OF THE sunniest places in New Zealand, so it's no wonder that more than 300 full-time artists and craftspeople have chosen to work in the area. The beautiful scenery and thriving arts scene prompted Robert and Sally Hunt, transplanted Americans, to put down roots here. Amid green hills, orchards, and vineyards about 40 miles from town, they built the luxurious Lodge at Paratiho Farms and planted its grounds with sculptures. Inside, vibrant canvases dominate the walls, and every horizontal surface is a possible showcase for a luminous glass bowl or a strikingly spare ceramic vase. The Hunts' enthusiasm is infectious, and they are generous about sharing their access to the arts community: you comment about a particular painting and before you know

Sunny Disposition

ON THE ARTS TRAIL, NELSON

Creative community: From the intricate stitches on a fantastic sea-goddess costume to the energetic strokes of an artist's paintbrush, inspiration abounds in Nelson.

it the artist has been invited to dinner. In the meantime, you head off to catch some of Nelson's laid-back vibes at the Saturday market on Montgomery Square, where holistic healers offer their services alongside a hodgepodge of stands selling everything from organic produce and fresh flowers to elaborate hand-stitched masks and handcrafted candles. After a few hours of gallery-hopping and shopping, you muster up whatever energy's left to visit Jane Evans, one of Nelson's most notable artists, at the Victorian-era garden cottage where she paints watery images that reflect her love of Chagall and Fauvist art. She leads you across a narrow lane to the guest house she rents out, a Victorian with a private garden and views across the bay. You can see why Jane isn't going anywhere. "Life here is really quite perfect. The light, the sea, nature, and flowers give me all the inspiration I need," she says. You nod, already planning to come and stay the next time you visit.

This quirky coastal town is hard to resist; don't be surprised if you find yourself drawn in by its welcoming cafés, one-of-a-kind shops, colorful markets, waterfront setting, and mellow pace.

BEAMS OF INTENSE SUNLIGHT TOUCH DOWN AROUND THE BEECHES, LANDING ON the path in front of you and, below, on a bay where cerulean waters lick at a gilt border of powdery sand. Summer's scent—crushed leaves and moist earth mixed with a touch of honeysuckle—is intoxicating, and the hum of cicadas has the effect of a meditative chant. Could there be a more beautiful spot for a swim? You think not, but like a strand of luminescent pearls, a string of other shimmering coves adorns the winding 32-mile coastal track in Abel Tasman National Park. Each sparkling inlet provokes a double take (is this the Caribbean? or an open-air set for *The Blue Lagoon*). "We get that a lot, except we can't get Brooke Shields here all the time," Darryl Wilson says with a grin, in between old tales of his family, whose history in the area goes back to the 1870s. Darryl guides walkers in the park, which is named for the first European,

Meandering by the Sea

WALKING THE ABEL TASMAN NATIONAL PARK TRACK

The endlessly absorbing coastal landscape offers a succession of idyllic beaches, glimmering coves, forest waterfalls, and crystal-clear lagoons.

a Dutchman, to sight New Zealand, in 1642. Walking the track is a commitment of three to five days, depending on your whim or speed. You can immerse yourself in the changing landscape of the bush; take to a sea kayak and explore the outer shores on the lookout for dolphins; or flop down on a soft beach to sunbathe before cooling off in a crystalline lagoon. By dusk, muscles thoroughly exhausted, you're ready to tuck into a meal at the beachfront lodge where you have a room. Tonight, Darryl's brother Craig, a chef, has fresh steamed mussels in white wine. Afterward, you amble happily up to bed. Within the space of a day you've been converted to "bush time," and you're in no hurry to return to life outside the park.

From curving shoreline to sunlit track,
the freedom of an unhampered stride, the
meditation of motion, the cicada's hum,
the sparkling clarity of transparent azure
seas: it's all a balm for the restless soul.

All the Details

Two main islands and a sprinkling of smaller ones make up New Zealand, or Aotearoa (Land of the Long White Cloud), as the Maori know this country in the South Pacific Ocean about 1,400 miles off the coast of Australia. Overall, it encompasses the same landmass as California but has a population of fewer than 4 million. The North Island is mostly subtropical, with idyllic, beach-lined, watery playgrounds to the north and a central volcanic plateau; the South Island is more rugged, with fjords, glaciers, and rain forests; daily temperature swings tend to be greater here. Regardless of season, steady, if not torrential, rain is likely along the South Island's west coast and in Fiordland. The December–March period is the warmest. February usually offers the best summer weather and is the most popular for visitors.

Auckland is 17 hours ahead of New York without daylight savings time. The two international airports are in Auckland and Christchurch; Wellington, the capital, and Queenstown are both regional hubs. Qantas (tel. 800/227–4500) and Air New Zealand (tel. 800/262–1234) offer daily nonstop Auckland–Los Angeles flights. Qantas also flies to Los Angeles from New York three times a week and code shares with American Airlines; Air New Zealand code shares with United Airlines. The flight from New York to Auckland takes about 19 hours; from Los Angeles, it's about 12 hours nonstop. For domestic flights, Air New Zealand and Air New Zealand Link (tel. 09/357–3000) are the main carriers. The longest domestic flight, between Auckland and Queenstown, takes only an hour and 15 minutes.

Buses and trains are reliable ways to get around, especially in the main cities. The New Zealand Travelpass (tel. 0800/339–966, www.travelpass.co.nz) includes travel on all four Tranz Scenic (tel. 0800/802–802) trains, the Interislander and Lynx ferry services, and InterCity and Newmans coach lines; the pass also can include air travel. Ferries shuttle between Wellington and Picton; the journey takes 3½ hours aboard the Interislander or two hours aboard the Lynx, a hydrofoil that sails only in calm weather. New Zealand is ideal for touring by car, as long as you can remember to drive on the left. Arrange a rental before you leave home.

This section provides the nitty-gritty information for each escape and is arranged geographically. Unless otherwise stated, properties are open year-round and accept credit cards, and rooms have private bathrooms. Prices are given in New Zealand dollars (the exchange rate at this writing is NZ$2.22 to US$1); they may or may not include GST (12.5%). When phoning or faxing from the United States, dial 011 plus 64 (the country code), then the number, dropping the initial zero that is

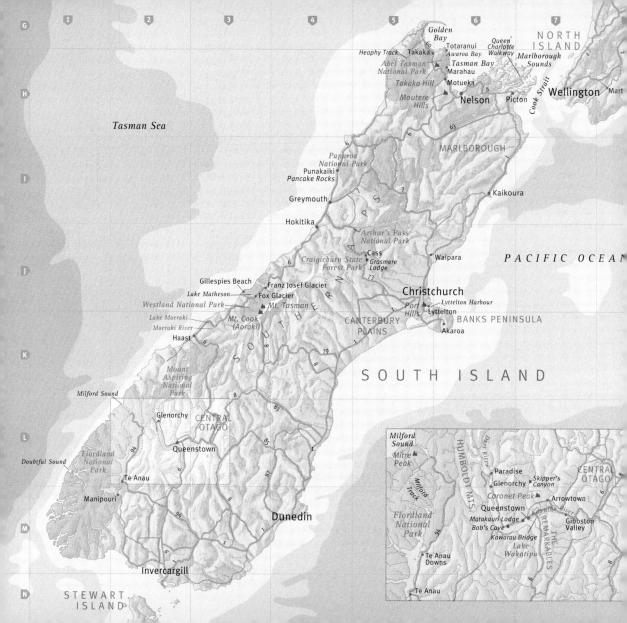

G ¹ ² ³ ⁴ ⁵ ⁶ ⁷

Golden Bay

NORTH ISLAND

Heaphy Track Takaka *Totaranui* *Queen Charlotte Walkway* *Marlborough Sounds*

Abel Tasman National Park *Awaroa Bay* *Tasman Bay* Marahau

Takaka Hill Motueka

H *Moutere Hills* Nelson Picton Wellington Mart.

Cook Strait

MARLBOROUGH

Tasman Sea

Paparoa National Park Punakaiki *Pancake Rocks*

I Kaikoura

Greymouth

Hokitika *Arthur's Pass National Park*

Cass Waipara

Craigieburn State Forest Park *Grasmere Lodge*

J Gillespies Beach Franz Josef Glacier Christchurch PACIFIC OCEAN

Lake Matheson Fox Glacier *Lyttelton Harbour*

Westland National Park Mt. Tasman Port Hills Lyttelton

Lake Moeraki Mt. Cook (Aoraki) CANTERBURY PLAINS BANKS PENINSULA

Moeraki River Akaroa

K Haast

Mount Aspiring National Park SOUTH ISLAND

Milford Sound

L Glenorchy CENTRAL OTAGO

Queenstown *Milford Sound*

Doubtful Sound *Fiordland National Park* *Mitre Peak* Paradise *Skipper's Canyon* CENTRAL OTAGO

Te Anau Glenorchy

Milford Track HUMBOLDT MTS. *Coronet Peak* Arrowtown

M Manipouri Queenstown *Kawarau River* Gibbston Valley

Dunedin *Fiordland National Park* *Matakauri Lodge* *Bob's Cove*

Kawarau Bridge *Lake Wakatipu* THE REMARKABLES

Te Anau Downs

N Invercargill Te Anau

STEWART ISLAND

required when dialing within the country. The tourism board's official Web site is www.purenz.com.

Grid coordinates, listed in parentheses after town names in the following section, refer to the maps on pages 79 and 80.

THE AUCKLAND REGION

New Zealand's largest city, Auckland (7C) is a cosmopolitan, creative pastiche of Maori, Polynesian, and European cultures. With a population of about 1 million, it sprawls across an isthmus that cinches the North Island's upper torso like a corset. The landscape is dominated by Waitemata Harbor (10–11B), which extends eastward to the island-dotted Hauraki Gulf (7–8C), and looming Rangitoto (11B), one of some 60 dormant and extinct volcanoes in the area. At the city's south edge, Manakau Harbor (10B–C) stretches west to the Tasman Sea and north toward the Waitakere Ranges (9–10B). Aucklanders take full advantage of the city's prime waterside location: the per-capita number of sailboats here is the highest of any city in the world. You can get around on foot in much of the core city—from Viaduct Harbor to such pleasant, café- and shop-filled areas as Ponsonby, Freemans Bay, Parnell, and Devonport—but you may need to take a bus, car, or ferry between neighborhoods. Don't miss the scenic walkways along Tamaki Drive and the North Shore bays; you'll easily see why Auckland is nicknamed City of Sails.

A COTTAGE STAY ON AUCKLAND'S WILD WEST COAST *(9B)*
Beach of Black Sand & Mist, p. 8

After a 40-minute drive west of Auckland, through the lush Waitakere Ranges, and down a sandy driveway, you can be surveying the windswept sands of Bethells Beach (9B) from a private cottage. A stay here offers a taste of real New Zealand–style comfort, and you are left in peace. If you don't want to cook, you can arrange for prepared breakfasts and dinners. Other black-sand beaches nearby include moody Karekare (9C), where parts of *The Piano* were filmed, Piha (9B), and Muriwai (9B). The sea is fierce and unforgiving here, but these beaches also offer lagoons and other safe swimming spots. Still, you may see some swimmers taking their chances (Bethells Beach has surf patrol during the summer). Just inland are vast native forests where walking trails lead to giant kauri, *nikau* palm groves, waterfalls, and icy natural pools hidden behind rocks.

CONTACT: Bethells Beach Cottages, Box 95057, Swanson, Auckland, tel.09/810–9581, fax 09/810–8677, www.bethells beach.com. 1 2-bedroom cottage (Te Koinga); 1 studio-style cottage (Turehu).

DISTANCES: Bethells Beach is 30 mi (48 km) west of Auckland.

PRICES: Te Koinga Cottage: NZ$275 double, NZ$25 per additional person. Turehu Cottage: NZ$175 double, NZ$15 per additional person. 2-night minimum. Rates exclude GST.

OPTIONS: Longtime Auckland-area residents Trude and John Bethell-Paice, the owners of Bethells Beach Cottages, can recommend a slew of activities, including local walks, guided beach hikes and horse treks, and vineyards you can visit. Massage therapy also can be arranged. Many artists are based in the Waitakere region; the Art Out West Artists and Artisans Trail brochure, available from the Auckland Visitor's Center (287 Queen St., Auckland, tel. 09/979–2333), lists studios, galleries, and related venues. ParksLine (tel. 09/303–1530) has information about walks in the Waitakere Ranges. If you are wary of heading off into the bush by yourself, consider joining an organized excursion with **Bush and Beach** (tel. 0800/423–224 or 09/478–2882, www.bushandbeach.co.nz).

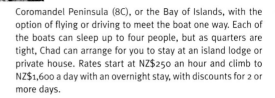

CRUISING THE ISLANDS OF THE HAURAKI GULF *(7–8C)*
A Sail Set into the Blue, p. 58

Sailing is a passion for Aucklanders, as well as for many other New Zealanders—the country has had scores of yacht-race successes, including America's Cup wins in 1995 and 2000—so it's easy to catch the bug yourself here. The *Ranui,* built in the early 1930s by a Norwegian whaling captain in self-exile on Stewart Island (2N), has served as an oyster dredger and a spy ship, among other things. These days it's perfect for exploring the Hauraki Gulf (7–8C) and its outlying islands, including Waiheke (11–12B), Rakino (11A), and Tiritiri Matangi (7C), a bird sanctuary. The cabins are plush and cozy, with flowers, hurricane lamps, fluffy towels, and portholes. Fishing rods, wet suits, and snorkeling gear are kept on board; you also can use the Hobie catamaran, 12-ft sailing dinghy, and Windsurfer. Longer charter trips can be arranged to the Bay of Islands (7B) or the Poor Knights Marine Reserve (7B), which the late Jacques Cousteau called one of the world's greatest diving areas.

CONTACT: Ranui South Pacific Charters, Box 47432, Ponsonby, Auckland, tel. 025/892–824, www.ranui.co.nz. 6 cabins (sleeps up to 14), 3 with private bathrooms.

DISTANCES: Hauraki Gulf is 1 1/4 mi (2 km) from Auckland.

PRICES: Full-boat charter (up to 14 people) NZ$1,995 a day, excluding drinks and meals; lunch cruise NZ$75 a person; full-day cruise NZ$99 a person; three-day cruise NZ$500 a person. Rates exclude GST.

OPTIONS: To test your boating skills aboard a classic 1930s yacht (smaller than the *Ranui*), contact Chad Thompson, a founding member of the Classic Yacht Association of New Zealand, at **New Zealand Classic Yachts Ltd.** (Box 147090, Ponsonby, Auckland, tel. 09/378–6271, fax 09/378–6281, www.classicyachtnz.com). Three vintage beauties are available for skippered charter: *Prize, Tawera,* and *Lady Gay* (a motor yacht). You can head out to Waiheke for lunch, or make overnight trips to other Hauraki Gulf islands, the Coromandel Peninsula (8C), or the Bay of Islands, with the option of flying or driving to meet the boat one way. Each of the boats can sleep up to four people, but as quarters are tight, Chad can arrange for you to stay at an island lodge or private house. Rates start at NZ$250 an hour and climb to NZ$1,600 a day with an overnight stay, with discounts for 2 or more days.

STAYING AT LONGHOUSE, WAIHEKE ISLAND *(11–12B)*
Island Aerie, p. 28

Waiheke, a popular weekend destination for Aucklanders, has a bohemian feel to it. Its small towns, including Oneroa, Onetangi, and Palm Beach (11B), brim with art studios, cafés, and organic-produce stores. Airy and uncluttered, Longhouse (11B) offers full immersion in Waiheke style at its most inspired. Three- to five-day cooking programs are regularly held here, with some one-day sessions offered, but Longhouse is just as appealing for short, recharging breaks. Even if you don't take part in the classes, food is a big part of the appeal. "Organic is best" tends to be the philosophy, and everything is super fresh. You can opt to have meals in the privacy of your room or take a picnic lunch to a white-sand beach. Work up your appetite exploring well-marked wilderness trails—on foot, mountain bike, scooter, horseback, or in a jeep—or boutique vineyards.

CONTACT: Longhouse, 155 Nick Johnstone Dr., Church Bay, Waiheke Island, Auckland, tel. 09/372–9619, fax 09/372–2537, www.longhousenz.com; 3 rooms. The Waiheke Visitor Information Center (Artworks, Box 96, Oneroa, tel. 09/372–9999, www.waiheke.co.nz) has general information about the island, including transportation, rentals, wine and art-studio tours, kayaking, horseback riding, and the annual Easter jazz festival. **Fullers ferry company** (tel. 09/376–9111) regularly makes the 35-minute crossing from Auckland's downtown Quay Street terminal to Waiheke Island's Matiatia wharf, where taxis and shuttles are available (or can be reserved).

DISTANCES: Waiheke Island is 12 nautical mi from downtown Auckland.

PRICES: NZ$450 double, NZ$400 single. Rates include full breakfast, a three-course dinner with wine, and GST; breakfast-only rates can be arranged. Cooking classes start at about NZ$260 for a one-day session.

OPTIONS: Don't miss lunch or dinner at **Te Whau Vineyard** (Te Whau Point, Te Whau Peninsula, tel. 09/372–7191), which overlooks the harbor out to Rangitoto and the city. Complementing the superb contemporary menu of dishes such as chorizo-wrapped Nelson Bay scallops, is a list of some 500 wines that focuses on selections from New Zealand and France. Wine-makers here say that because the island's climate—a few degrees warmer than on the mainland—is similar to that of Bordeaux, the soil is ideal for growing cabernet and merlot grapes as well as olives, which are pressed into oil. To visit the island's 29 vineyards, you can follow the Waiheke Winegrowers Map, available at the island visitor center. **Goldwater Estate** (18 Causeway Rd., Putiki Bay, tel. 09/372–7493), the first vineyard established on the island, is a must for its idyllic setting and its wines (they've won prestigious awards and have an international following). In summer the winery is open daily 11–4; tours and tastings are by appointment only. The **Mudbrick** (Church Bay Road, Oneroa, tel. 09/372–9050) and **Stonyridge** (80 Onetangi Rd., tel. 09/372–8822) vineyards are also worth visiting for tastings; plus, both have restaurants with alfresco dining and lovely views. **Miro Vineyard** (Browns Rd., tel. 09/372–7854, fax 09/372–7056, miro@xtra.co.nz; NZ$175) is a Tuscan-style hillside villa above a valley of grapevines that overlooks Onetangi Beach (11B). The property includes a private rental house with a kitchen and deck, or you can opt for bed-and-breakfast accommodation in the main house. **17 Pah Road** (17 Pah Rd., Onetangi, tel. 09/372–7571, fax 09/ 372–7571, pahroad@xtra.co.nz; NZ$250, 2-night minimum) offers a contemporary studio-style bungalow with a large deck overlooking Onetangi Beach; the owners throw in use of a four-wheel-drive Suzuki.

THE PASIFIKA FESTIVAL, AUCKLAND *(10–11B)*
Woven Strands of Polynesia, p. 14

To many of its Pacific Islanders, Auckland is *Tamaki makaurau,* the first city of the Pacific; it has the largest Polynesian population in the world. The annual one-day **Pasifika Festival,** usually held in early March, celebrates Pacific Island cultures, notably those of Samoa, Tonga, Niue, Tokelau, Tuvalu, Fiji, and the Cook Islands, all with large communities in Auckland. Music is a major part of the festival, New Zealand's biggest with more than 100,000 attendees. Performances feature such top acts as the Pacific Music Ensemble, the Yandall Sisters, the rap singers Che Fu and King Kapesi, and Faux Nature, as well as Cook Island ukulele bands. Several Pacific Island communities perform traditional kava ceremonies, accompanied by conch calls and various rituals honoring local *matai,* or chieftains.

CONTACT: Auckland Event Line (tel. 09/379–1352, www. akcity.govt.nz/pasifika) can provide details about the festival.

OPTIONS: Another way you can absorb the flavor of Auckland's Pacific Island community is by walking **Karangahape Road,** lined with specialty produce markets and shops. **Buana Satu** (229 Karangahape Rd., Newton, Auckland, tel. 09/358–5561) sells fun Tongan tapa, kitschy hula skirts, and funky T-shirts. Or seek out a game of *kilikiti,* the Samoan version of cricket, easily distinguished from cricket by the colorful *lava-lava,* or sarong-like wraps, the men wear around their whites; games are held in large parks all over Auckland in December and January. If you wish to attend a traditional church service, just pick a Pacific Islander church. Most Auckland neighborhoods have at least one; some, such as Ponsonby and Grey Lynn, have as many as 10. The services are musical and give you the chance to see communities in their Sunday finery: big flowery hats, dresses with identical clan-style patterns, men in formal woven skirts. Be prepared to stay afterwards—you might be invited to lunch.

A MAORI RENAISSANCE
The Sacred Breath, p. 38

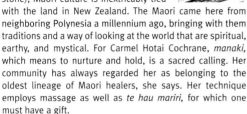

Like the tears etched on *pounamu* (greenstone), Maori culture is inextricably tied with the land in New Zealand. The Maori came here from neighboring Polynesia a millennium ago, bringing with them traditions and a way of looking at the world that are spiritual, earthy, and mystical. For Carmel Hotai Cochrane, *manaki,* which means to nurture and hold, is a sacred calling. Her community has always regarded her as belonging to the oldest lineage of Maori healers, she says. Her technique employs massage as well as *te hau mariri,* for which one must have a gift.

There are many ways for you to experience and learn about Maori traditions. You can hear the spine-chilling *wero* (a formal welcoming challenge always led by a top warrior at a *marae,* or Maori meeting place), meet Maori in their homes, and see the best of Maori art and architecture, especially in Rotorua and in the more Maori-populous North Island. The **Auckland Memorial War Museum** (tel. 09/309–0443) has one of the most impressive collections of Maori *taonga* (treasures) in the country; the **Mataoroa Art Gallery** (tel. 09/360–0636), also in Auckland, is a good place to seek out contemporary Maori art and fine jewelry, as well as to chat with its Maori owners. In Wellington (7H), the modern, interactive **Te Papa–Museum of New Zealand** (tel. 04/381–7100) is a must for its Maori-related exhibits, and the **National Tattoo Museum** (tel. 04/385–6446) is dedicated to the history of the traditional Maori *ta moko* (tattoo), which can be thought of as a sort of wearable *whakapapa,* or ancestral knowledge.

CONTACT: Carmel Hotai, **Manaki Bodywork Clinic,** 887 Dominion Rd., Balmoral, tel. 09/620–2635, fax 09/620–2631.

PRICES: NZ$80–NZ$140 for 1–1½ hrs., depending on the treatment.

OPTIONS: Red Feather/Tia Raukura Expeditions (contact Beth Coleman, Box 60243, Titirangi, Auckland, tel./fax 09/817–9396, www.ecotoursnz.com) creates cultural and natural heritage tours of New Zealand, which can include meeting with Maori teachers and other specialists on such topics as performing arts, astronomy, and healing. A big event on the Maori calendar is the **Kapa Haka Festival,** the Aotearoa Traditional Maori Performing Arts Festival held in February in even-numbered years. The three-day event showcases the country's best *haka* (war dance) and music performances, and includes craft and food stalls and *ta moko* demonstrations. Contact **Aotearoa Traditional Maori Performing Arts Society** (tel. 04/499–6158 or 0800/188–071, fax 04/499–6159, www.kapahaka.org.nz) for the next location and other details. Useful Web sites relating to Maori culture include maori.culture.com, www.maori.org.nz, tamoko.org.nz, and creativenz.govt.nz.

AUCKLAND REGION HIGHLIGHTS

The **Bay of Islands,** a sensuous, subtropical island-dotted region of beaches, farms, and forests, is a three-hour drive from Auckland. Make pretty **Russell** (7B) your base. One of New Zealand's first European settlements, it has a tree-lined promenade, historic museums, and Victorian-era B&Bs. In **Waitangi** (7B), a 3-mi ferry ride across the bay, a treaty granting the British sovereignty was signed in 1840; the Maori have disputed the treaty ever since. It's worthwhile to stroll the grounds of the former British Resident's home, the Treaty House, and to see its impressive *marae* (Maori meeting place) and ceremonial *waka,* or canoe. Farther north are the wild, white-sand beaches of the **Karikari Peninsula** (6A) and the fishing village of **Mangonui** (6A). At the tip of North Island are the rolling sand dunes of **Ninety Mile Beach** (5–6A) and **Cape Reinga** (5A) — in Maori legend, the send-off point for Maori souls departing for the mythical homeland of Hawaiki. Looping back to Auckland via Highway 12 puts you on the west coast and through **Waipoua Forest** (6B), with its majestic 1,200-year-old kauri trees.

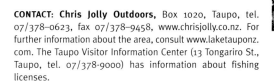

CENTRAL NORTH ISLAND

Pastoral hills and rugged wilderness areas alternate with surreal volcanic and thermal scenery in the central North Island, home to one-third of the country's Maori population. The local Te Arawa Maori believed this landscape was the handiwork of gods who were both benevolently creative and furiously destructive. In 1886, the most devastating of the country's recent volcanic explosions ripped apart and rearranged the Rotorua lakes region (8E) into smoldering geothermal valleys; today angry geysers and sulfur-belching mud pools characterize the region. Lake Taupo (8E–F), the country's largest lake, sits in the center of the North Island; easily visible from it is Mount Ruapehu (8F), the centerpiece of Tongariro National Park (8F–G) and, at 9,175 ft, the island's tallest peak. The mysterious forests of Te Urewera National Park (9E) lie on the island's east side.

FLY-FISHING THE TONGARIRO-TAUPO RIVER *(8F)*
The Lure of the Trout, p. 42

The Taupo region is considered by many to offer the finest brown- and rainbow-trout fishing anywhere, and its crystalline rivers, streams, and pumice-beach lakes are spectacularly scenic. During the winter spawning runs into the tributary streams of Lake Taupo, icy waters prompt some 750,000 prime rainbows averaging five pounds and often twice that size to make their way upriver. Equally impressive is that these fish aren't stocked—they all come from wild reserves. Although you can fish year-round, winter is best for river and lake fishing; summer offers the distinct challenge of "stalking the fish" in the clear waters (with visibility of more than 30 ft) found high in the mountain ranges and reached only by helicopter. You're allowed to catch a maximum of three fish a day. Plus, in order to eat trout in this part of the world, you have to catch it yourself, or know someone who has.

CONTACT: Chris Jolly Outdoors, Box 1020, Taupo, tel. 07/378-0623, fax 07/378-9458, www.chrisjolly.co.nz. For further information about the area, consult www.laketauponz.com. The Taupo Visitor Information Center (13 Tongariro St., Taupo, tel. 07/378-9000) has information about fishing licenses.

DISTANCES: Entrance to the main tributary streams off the Tongariro-Taupo River is 19 mi (30 km) southwest of Taupo (8E).

PRICES: A one-day license to fish in the Taupo region is NZ$12; if you hire a guide, he files the paperwork for you. A full day with one of Chris Jolly's specialist fly-fishing guides usually costs NZ$675, which covers all gear and can include a picnic basket. There may be some room for negotiation, depending on the size of your party and time of year; half-day rates are another possibility.

OPTIONS: As popular with honeymooners as it is with anglers, the **Huka Lodge** property (Huka Falls Road, Box 95, Taupo, tel. 07/378-5791, fax 07/378-0427, www.hukalodge.com; NZ$895 double per person, January–March) overlooks the fast-flowing, gin-clear Waikato River (8D–E), just ahead of the Huka Falls. Lush gardens, a hot tub, and a petanque court are outside; inside, the look is faux rustic. Expect a little formality here. Accommodations are in 20 suites (double or twin share) and a three-bedroom cottage. The rates include pre-dinner drinks, a five-course dinner, breakfast, and Taupo Airport transfers.

HIKING TONGARIRO CROSSING, TONGARIRO NATIONAL PARK *(8F)*
Among the Volcanoes, p. 62

Tongariro was the country's first national park, donated in 1887 to the people of New Zealand by a Maori chief and still considered sacred to the Maori. Southwest of Taupo, the park is dominated by three active volcanoes: Tongariro (8F), Ngauruhoe (8F), and Ruapehu. Walking the Tongariro Crossing

takes 7 to 8 hours. You need to be fairly fit for the walk, much of which involves steep climbs up and down hills. Even in midsummer you should anticipate sudden weather changes; bring a waterproof raincoat, sturdy boots, sunscreen, and sunglasses, as well as food and plenty of beverages—drinking water isn't available along the track. For winter conditions, including snow, you need special gear, such as an ice ax and crampons. The track starts at Mangatepopo (8F), off Highway 47, a short distance from Whakapapa Village (8F).

CONTACT: Outdoor Experiences (597 Valle Rd., RD 1, Reporoa, tel. 07/333–7099 or 0800/806–369, fax 07/333–8635, www.outdoorexperiencesnz.com) is the only company licensed by the Department of Conservation as guides for the Tongariro Crossing. The Whakapapa Visitors Center (Hwy. 48, Mount Ruapehu, tel. 07/892–3729, www.doc.govt.nz) has displays about the park, as well as helpful trekking and skiing advice; it's also a good place to buy maps, guides, and some equipment. A shuttle bus run by **Tongariro Track Transport** (tel. 07/892–3897) leaves the Whakapapa Visitors Center at 8 a.m. and picks up at Ketetahi (8F) at 4:30 or 6 p.m.

DISTANCES: Tongariro National Park is 68 mi (110 km) southwest of Taupo.

OPTIONS: Built in 1929 in French-château style, the **Grand Chateau** (Hwy. 48, Mount Ruapehu, Tongariro National Park, tel. 07/892–3809, fax 07/892–3704, www.chateau.co.nz; NZ$125–NZ$195, including GST) dominates the otherwise empty volcano-ringed landscape as you drive up through Tongariro National Park's vast tussock-pocked expanse.

TE UREWERA NATIONAL PARK (9E)
The Realm of the Tuhoe, p. 26

If you plan to rough it and sleep outdoors, expect no more than basic facilities. The reward is the spectacular beauty of this vast forested wilderness straddling the remote Huiarau Range (9E). Lake Waikaremoana (9E), "sea of rippling waters," is the park's centerpiece; dense native forest and waterfalls tumble to the water's edge, and the dramatic Panekiri Bluff (9F) towers over its southern shores. Especially popular in summer for swimming, fishing, and boating, the lake is circled by a 31-mi (50-km) track; the three- to four-day walk is regarded as one of the country's finest. You need to book ahead to stay at the camping huts along the track. A private shuttle and water-taxi service can ferry you to major sections of the walk and pick you up by arrangement. Plenty of shorter walks start at the Visitors Center; one to Lake Waikareiti (9E), about an hour each way, leads you through *rimu* and silver beech forest. You can hire a rowboat to reach small Rahui Island and its unusual lake-on-an-island-in-a-lake, which you climb up a ladder to find. Access to Lake Waikaremoana is via the largely unpaved Highway 38 from Murupara (9E), after turning off the Rotorua-Taupo Highway 5. Alternatively, there is access from Wairoa (9F), 62 mi (100 km) southwest of Gisborne (10E), along Highway 2.

CONTACT: Aniwaniwa Visitors Center, Department of Conservation, Te Urewera National Park, Private Bag 2213, Wairoa, tel. 06/837–3900 or 06/837–3803, fax 06/837–3722, www.doc.govt.nz/explore/. **Te Urewera Adventures** (Ruatahuna, Box 3001, Rotorua, tel. 07/366–3969, fax 07/366–3333, biddlemarg@clear.net.nz) is a Maori-owned company that leads horse-trekking/camping expeditions through the Te Urewera ranges. **Waikaremoana Guided Tours** (Te Kairere, Tuai, Wairoa, tel. 06/837–3729) offers ferry, water-taxi, and shuttle service to points along the Lake Waikaremoana walk and other locations. For other information about Lake Waikaremoana, check www.lake.co.nz.

DISTANCES: Lake Waikaremoana is 60 mi (97 km) east of Murupara and 101 mi (163 km) west of Gisborne.

OPTIONS: Nestled on the lakeshore, the **Waikaremoana Motor Camp** (Te Urewera National Park, Private Bag 2058, Wairoa, tel. 06/837–3826, fax 06/837–3825; NZ$68–NZ$120, including GST) is a little haven of civilization amid otherwise complete isolation. Lodging choices here include family

units and lakeside "fishermen's cabins." Judy Doyle's **Waikaremoana Homestay** (RD 5, Wairoa, tel. 06/837–3701, fax 06/837–3709, ykarestay@xtra.co.nz; NZ$80, including GST), near Lake Waikaremoana, offers B&B accommodations in the mostly Tuhoe settlement of Tuai (9E), with dinner by arrangement.

CENTRAL NORTH ISLAND HIGHLIGHTS
In Rotorua, a winding trail leads you past swirling mud pools and steaming geysers in **Whakarewarewa** (8E) to a reconstructed Maori village with an arts-and-crafts center where carvers and weavers work. A 15-minute drive south of Rotorua on the Taupo highway is the **Tamaki Maori Village** (8E), a commercialized version of the real thing that affords you an organized feel-good immersion in Maori culture. You may want a more authentic stay on a marae; not only will you be welcomed with a *powhiri* ceremony, which involves the warrior-like *wero* challenge and a *karanga* (call of welcome by a local woman), but you probably will find yourself being led on late-night expeditions in search of outdoor hot pools. The ceremony and an authentic meal cost NZ$65; an overnight stay (including breakfast) is NZ$130 per person. Contact **Rotoiti Tours** (Box 862, Rotorua, tel. 0800/476–864, rotoiti@voyager.co.nz) for details.

WELLINGTON AND THE WAIRARAPA

Its reputation for strong gales and correspondingly stoical temperaments notwithstanding, Wellington, New Zealand's capital, has been emerging as the island's most cosmopolitan city, winning an edge over Auckland with its dynamic arts and restaurant scenes. At the south tip of the North Island, Wellington is the embarkation point for the South Island ferry. The Wairarapa (7H–8G), an hour's drive north over the Rimutaka Range (7–8H)—referred to by Wellingtonians as "the Hill"—has a wild coast with dramatic windswept limestone cliffs and excellent wineries.

A FESTIVAL OF FOOD, WINE, AND MUSIC IN WAIRARAPA *(8H)*
Toast Martinborough, p. 66

In the wine-growing world, New Zealand's cool, maritime climate often draws comparison with Burgundy and Bordeaux as well as Oregon. Although the Marlborough Valley sauvignon blancs are the best known of the country's wines, there are many other wine-producing areas to explore, namely Hawkes Bay (9–10F), Central Otago (2–3L), Waiheke (11–12B), and, especially, Martinborough (8H). Since the 1990s, Martinborough's community of passionate, artisanal-minded wine-makers has been producing some of the best wine in the country and making a name among pinot noirs. The staff at the Martinborough Wine Center, in the heart of town, can help you plan a wine tour and offer tastings of Wairarapa wines as well as pinot noirs from around the world. The Wairarapa Growers Market, held at the center Saturday until noon, sells produce.

CONTACT: Tourism Martinborough, 18 Kitchener St., Martinborough, tel. 06/306–9043, fax 06/306–8033. Two Web sites, www.toastmartinborough.co.nz and www.nzwine.com, also have information about Toast Martinborough, which is usually held the third Sunday in November. **Martinborough Wine Center** (tel. 06/306–9040, fax 06/306–9070). For train service to and from Wellington, contact Tranz Metro (tel. 04/498–3000 ext. 43103).

DISTANCES: Martinborough is 52 mi (84 km) north of Wellington.

OPTIONS: Other wine festivals of note include **Harvest Hawkes Bay** (www.hawkesbaytourism.co.nz/events.asps), held the first week of February, and **Toast Marlborough** (www.winemarlboroughfestival.co.nz), held the second Saturday in February. Consult www.wineinthepacific.com for more information. The **Martinborough Fair**—a traditional village fair with arts, crafts, music, food, and wine—is held the first Saturday in March; the **Scarecrow Festival** is held in nearby Gladstone (8H) between late October and late

November. Tourism Martinborough has information about both events. In town, many of the 11 bedrooms in the restored 1882 **Martinborough Hotel** (The Square, Martinborough, tel. 06/306–9350, fax 06/306–9345, www.martinboroughhotel.co.nz; NZ$240–NZ$295, including GST) have claw-foot tubs. The hotel bistro uses local produce and offers more than 100 pinot noirs. On the rugged Palliser Bay (7H), about a 40-minute drive from Martinborough, or a one-hour drive from Wellington, is the ultra-luxurious **Wharekauhau Country Estate** (Western Lake Road, Palliser Bay, RD 3, Featherston, tel. 06/307–7581, fax 06/307–7799, www.wharekauhau.co.nz; NZ$735 double per person or NZ $955 single, including breakfast, aperitifs, and a four-course dinner). Set on a 5,000-acre sheep station, it overlooks a black-sand coast and the purple-hued Rimutaka Mountains. Four cottages house 10 spacious suites, each with a fireplace, fully stocked bar, and private veranda. The views of the Pacific, especially from the three Stormwatch cottages, are mesmerizing. Rates exclude GST.

WELLINGTON HIGHLIGHTS
Wellington is easy to navigate on foot, although its often-steep hills are not for the faint-hearted. Take the Kelburn Cable Car to the **Wellington Botanic Garden,** which gives you fine city views on one side, and then saunter to the **Lady Norwood Rose Garden** and the charming Victorian-era neighborhood of Thorndon, off Tinakori Road. Tucked away at 25 Tinakori Road is the **Katherine Mansfield House,** where the celebrated writer was born and spent her early childhood years. Walking along the harbor from Queen's Wharf, you pass bars and restaurants on the way **Civic Square** and its intriguing collection of sculptures. **Oriental Bay,** with its promenade of monkey puzzle trees, a small beach, and wooden houses, offers a whiff of old Wellington. The biennial **New Zealand International Festival of the Arts** (www.nzfestival.telecom.co.nz), the country's most celebrated cultural event, attracts artists, performers, writers, and audiences from around the world. It's held in even years, usually around late February to mid-March.

UPPER SOUTH ISLAND
The difference between the south and the north islands is subtle but almost alchemical. On the South Island, everything is bigger, more majestic and open-spaced, from the glacial lakes and towering mountain ranges to the spectacular coastline with whale-sojourning areas to the east and dramatic fjords to the west. At the island's north end are the sunshine-filled regions of Nelson (6H) and the Marlborough Sounds (6G–7H), dotted with maritime and inland national parks, including the coastal Abel Tasman National Park (6H), as well as Marlborough (6I–7H), the famous wine-producing region.

ON THE ARTS TRAIL, NELSON *(6H)*
Sunny Disposition, p. 68

Thanks to its abundance of sunshine, the Nelson area is full of orchards, vineyards, olive groves, herbs, and flowers of all kinds. The strong creative community is a major draw, as are the nearby beaches. Wine-making is a local passion, so there are numerous vineyards to visit. Visiting artists in their studios, sampling local wines in the rolling Moutere Hills (6H), unwinding by the sea, savoring deliciously fresh scallops and crayfish—what better way to spend a few days?

CONTACT: Nelson Tourism Services (284 Trafalgar St., Box 1282, Nelson) can arrange wine and art tours. The best guide to the Nelson art scene is *Art In Its Own Place,* available at the Nelson Visitor Information Center (corner of Trafalgar and Halifax Sts., Box 194, Nelson, tel. 03/548–2304, fax 03/546–7393, www.nelson.net.nz). **Winemakers of Nelson,** is on the Web at www.nzwine.com/nelson.

DISTANCES: Nelson is 263 mi (424 km) from Christchurch (5J).

OPTIONS: Admire the sculptural, fantastical garments at the **World of Wearable Art** (95 Quarantine Rd., Annesbrook, tel. 03/548–9299, www.worldofwearableart.com), open daily. **The Smokehouse** (Shed 3, Mapua Wharf, Nelson, tel. 03/540–2280) has a wonderful riverside setting that you can soak up during lunch; don't ignore the manuka-smoked fish platters and smoked eel. Another Nelson gem is the **Boatshed Café and Restaurant** (350 Wakefield Quay, Nelson, tel. 03/546–9783), with harbor views and fresh seafood. One highlight of the wine trail is **Denton Winery** (Awa Awa Road off Marriages Road, Coastal Highway, Nelson, tel./fax 03/540–355), set among park-like hills. It sells local cheeses and produce, handmade chutneys, and homemade breads and is open daily 11–5 4th weekend of Oct.–Easter. Nelson's **Saturday Market** is held from 8–1 in Montgomery Square. Jane Evans's **39 Russell Street** (39 Russell St., Nelson, tel. 03/548–4655, fax 03/548–4677, www.nelsonluxuryaccommodation.co.nz; NZ$350–NZ$400, 2-night minimum) is a colorful former fisherman's cottage with vibrant ceramics and Philippe Starck bathroom fixtures and a well-stocked larder. Across the road from the artist's home and studio, it offers privacy, independence, and harbor views. Outside of Nelson proper, the **Lodge at Paratiho Farms** (545 Waiwhero Rd., RD 2, Upper Moutere, Nelson, tel. 03/528–2100, fax 03/528–2101, www.paratiho.co.nz; NZ$ 1,850 per couple) has six private cottages, each with a suite and fireplace. Everything here says luxury: sumptuous Oriental rugs, antique Chinese chests, crystal vases, clawfoot tubs, and sheepskin bath rugs. The meals, prepared by chef Will van Heeswyck, are impeccable and inventive. The rate (which is discounted by NZ$250 for single occupancy but does not include GST), includes all meals and beverages, use of the facilities—including the pool, gym (equipped with state-of-the-art Pilates machines), and tennis court—and access to the health and beauty spa.

WALKING THE ABEL TASMAN NATIONAL PARK TRACK (6H)
Meandering by the Sea, p. 72

Whichever way you walk along the Abel Tasman National Park track—either north from Totaranui (6G) or south from Marahau (6H)—the trip takes 3–5 days, the perfect amount of time to soak up the ambience of this beautiful, tranquil coast. You can "freedom walk" the clearly signposted trail, arranging your own accommodation in advance, or opt for a guided walk. If you book a guided walk with Abel Tasman National Park Experiences, you stay at the company's two comfortable family-owned and -operated lodges. You also can arrange to boat to points along the track for just a day's trek and kayak if you wish. Most day walks take between two and six hours. Water-launch services can transport your luggage ahead, so that you can walk the track with only your basic necessities.

CONTACT: **Abel Tasman National Park Experiences,** Box 351, Motueka, Nelson, tel. 03/528–7801 or 0800/221–888, fax 03/528–6087, www.abeltasman.co.nz.

DISTANCES: Abel Tasman National Park is 48 mi (77 km) northwest of Motueka (6H) and 69 mi (110 km) northwest of Nelson.

PRICES: Depending on the season, rates for guided treks range from NZ$420 for 2 days to NZ$1,080–NZ$1,300 for 5 days, including meals, sea kayaking, shared twin accommodation, luggage transfer, transport to and from Motueka or Nelson, and GST.

OPTIONS: Freedom walkers have a few lodging options. **Abel Tasman Marahau Lodge** (Marahau, RD 2, Motueka, tel. 03/527–8250, fax 03/527–8258, www.abeltasmanmarahaulodge.co.nz; doubles from NZ$108) offers spacious rooms. **Awaroa Lodge and Café** (Abel Tasman National Park, Box 163, Takaka 7172, tel. 03/528–8758, fax 03/528–6561, www.awaroalodge.co.nz; NZ$125–NZ$135, including GST), set on spectacular Awaroa Bay (6H), has private cabins as well as standard doubles with shared facilities; it can be reached on foot or by boat. **Aqua Taxi** (tel. 03/527–8083) leaves daily from Marahau for Awaroa and other points along the trail. **Tasman Bay Aviation** (tel. 03/547–2378) flies between Nelson and the airstrip at Awaroa Lodge.

UPPER SOUTH ISLAND HIGHLIGHTS
From Nelson, head northward over **Takaka Hill** (5H), past its primitive-looking outcrops, to **Golden Bay** (5–6G), setting up base in the town of **Takaka,** with its colorful community of artists and craftspeople. Along the bay is **Totaranui Beach** (6G), one of the few beaches within Abel Tasman National Park that you can reach by road. Within the Nelson–Marlborough region, at the South Island's northern tip, you can explore the **Marlborough Sounds** by boat, walk the coastal **Queen Charlotte Walkway** (6–7H), take the **Heaphy track** (5G–H) from Golden Bay to the West Coast, and watch whales at **Kaikoura** (6I).

CHRISTCHURCH AND THE CENTRAL SOUTH ISLAND

Many people declare Christchurch (5J), which sits midway along the South Island's east coast, to be their favorite New Zealand city. Not only is Christchurch garden-obsessed, almost continually in bloom or full leaf, it's also manageable in size, has a strong arts-focused community, and somehow feels caught up with the world yet comfortably time-warped. The Canterbury Plains (4K–5J) countryside is to the west; Waipara (5J), the Banks Peninsula (6J–K), and the Southern Alps (3K–5I), encompassing Mount Cook (3K) and Arthur's Pass (5J–I), are all within 100 mi of the city.

PUNTING ON THE AVON, CHRISTCHURCH (5J)
An Edwardian River Glide, p. 48

Often described as the most English city outside England, Christchurch was founded in 1850 by the utopian-minded Canterbury Association, members of Christ Church College, Oxford, and presided over by the Archbishop of Canterbury. You don't want to be rushed here, whether you are admiring the profusion of magnolias and wild English roses, watching cricket on a Saturday morning, or quaffing a locally brewed ale in a Cotswoldian pub. A punt along the Avon, which threads through the city, fits in perfectly with this pace; tours leave on request from the Antigua Boatshed daily from 10 until dusk.

CONTACT: Punting in the Park, Antigua Boatshed, 2 Cambridge Terr., tel./fax 03/366–0337.

DISTANCES: Christchurch is 330 mi (528 km) northeast of Queenstown (2L).

PRICES: NZ$12.50, including use of blankets and cushions. Special candlelight and moonlight punts are available.

OPTIONS: A classic English-style garden city must have an elegant old lady of a hotel. The **Charlotte Jane** (110 Papanui Rd., tel. 03/355–1028, fax 03/355–8882, www.charlotte-jane.co.nz; NZ$235–NZ$340), once a private Victorian boarding school for young girls, is named for one of the first ships to bring the early European settlers to Canterbury. In your suite you can light a fire before climbing into the whirlpool bath and, later, into a bed draped with lacy linens and a Kashmir shawl. The intimate conservatory restaurant looks onto a garden. Rates include a deluxe breakfast, unlimited coffee and tea, and GST. Devonshire teas are best at **The Sign of the Kiwi** (Dyers Pass at Summit Road, on the Port Hills, tel. 03/329–9966; open daily 10–4), where the proprietor grows the berries for her homemade jam and bakes heavenly scones.

A STAY AT GRASMERE LODGE, CASS (5J)
Up at the Farm, p. 44

The drive from Christchurch to Grasmere Lodge (5J) becomes increasingly spectacular once you leave behind the green Canterbury Plains and climb up into the gigantic mountains with their many folds. Tucked away in the Southern Alps, the Grasmere Lodge property includes five lakes and three rivers; Arthur's Pass National Park borders one side, Craigieburn State Forest Park (4–5J) another. Owners Oliver and Vicki Newbegin restored the original 1858 limestone homestead and added a sublime heated pool, a hillside wine cellar, a wing with guest suites, and a leather-bound library. Meals are refined; expect local venison, lamb, and salmon, as well as whitebait from the West Coast, decadent desserts, and a sophisticated wine selection. With prior arrangement, the TranzAlpine train stops at Mount White Bridge for Grasmere guests. Nearby Cass (5J) was once a thriving 1880s staging-post settlement, a haunt of wayfarers and rogues, known as swagmen in these parts. These days, and for as long as anyone can remember, it has a resident population of just one, a man everyone for miles knows as "Barry."

CONTACT: Grasmere Lodge, Highway 73, Cass, Canterbury, Private Bag 55009, Christchurch, tel. 03/318–8407, fax 03/318–8263, www.grasmere.co.nz. 12 rooms.

DISTANCES: Grasmere Lodge is 73 miles (120 km) west of Christchurch.

PRICES: NZ$440 double–NZ$800 Grasmere suite; prices are per person and include pre-dinner New Zealand wine tasting and canapés, five-course dinner, and full breakfast, but exclude GST.

OPTIONS: Included in a stay at the Grasmere Lodge is a 90-minute four-wheel-drive tour of the property. You can also go for guided alpine walks and horse-riding treks, fly-fish for brown and rainbow trout, and lake kayak. Other activities include tennis, croquet, and boules, and you can try your hand at feeding the animals or shearing sheep.

A GUIDED WALK ON FOX GLACIER, WESTLAND NATIONAL PARK (3J)
Catacombs of Ice, p. 22

Plan on at least three hours up on the glaciers, with the choice of a morning or an afternoon expedition. Leave your car in the Alpine Guides Fox Glacier parking lot in Fox Glacier township (3J), then check into the company headquarters, where you are fitted with big woolen socks, 15-pound hob-nailed boots, and crampons. You must bring your own jacket, hat and gloves if it's chilly, sunscreen, and UV-protective sunglasses. A helicopter whisks you over the upper icefall and the cascading waters of Victoria Falls before landing in the remote ice fields. The climb travels about 1 ¼ mi (2 km) up the glacier and requires a reasonable level of fitness. This mighty river of ice meanders through the valley, descending into temperate rain forest and ending only 12 mi (20 km) from the Tasman Sea. Westland National Park (3J–4K) actually has 60 glaciers, formed by the intense deluges of rain on the West Coast, but the most famous and accessible are Fox and Franz Josef glaciers (3J).

CONTACT: Alpine Guides Fox Glacier, Box 38, Fox Glacier 7951, tel. 03/751–0825, fax 03/751–0857, www.foxguides. co.nz. Tours depart daily at 9 and noon Sept.–Apr., at 10:30 and 1:30 in May, and at noon in June; always check ahead for reporting times. All-day and overnight heli-hiking expeditions as well as guided mountain adventures are options.

DISTANCES: Fox Glacier is 106 mi (170 km) south of Hokitika (4J).

PRICES: NZ$195 for half day.

OPTIONS: You can always take in the impressive views up either of the glacier's flanks from viewing platforms and trails at the bottom of the glacier flow, in the parking areas outside the towns. Relax before or after your heli-hike at the **Wilderness Lodge Lake Moeraki** (Highway 6, Haast, tel. 03/750–0881, fax 03/750–0882, www.wildernesslodge.co.nz;

NZ$185–NZ$240), on the bank of the Moeraki River (3K). Set amid spectacular remote rain forest within the Westland National Park, the property gives you access to thousand-year-old native trees, rare Fiordland crested penguins, and seals; surrounding forests and walkways can be explored on foot or with a vehicle, kayak, or mountain bike. The rate includes breakfast, a four-course dinner, and GST.

CHRISTCHURCH AND CENTRAL SOUTH ISLAND HIGHLIGHTS

Within an easy hour's stroll you can cover most of the great sights in Christchurch: the magnificent **Botanic Gardens** and adjacent **Arts Centre** with its colorful weekend market, the **Roger McDougal Art Gallery,** and **Canterbury Museum.** The **Curator's House and Plant Garden,** the original Tudor-style cottage that belonged to the curator of the Botanic Gardens, has been made into a café–restaurant with Victorian-style potager gardens. For a quick overview of the city's architecture, including the 1894 cathedral, hop aboard a restored Victorian tram. If you have an afternoon, explore **Lyttelton** (5J), the small harbor town a few miles south, where the early Christchurch settlers first landed, and the **Port Hills** (5K), which offer stunning views over the city and the patchwork fields of the **Canterbury Plains.** Beyond that, take at least a couple of days to soak up the laid-back communities of the **Banks Peninsula,** where lavender-farming and cheese- and pottery-making are favored activities, and the seaside village of **Akaroa** (6K), founded by the French. From Christchurch you can also make your way up into **Arthur's Pass National Park** for an overland route across to the West Coast. Outside Fox Glacier township, don't miss the walking trail around beautiful **Lake Matheson** (3J), famous for its reflections of snow-capped Mount Cook/Aoraki (3K) and Mount Tasman (3J). **Gillespies Beach** (3J), with its crashing surf and seal colony, is 25 minutes away by car.

QUEENSTOWN AND FIORDLAND

Tucked inland in the South Island's western corner, Queenstown—with its reputation as the self-styled adrenaline capital of the world—is arranged around a sinuous curve of Lake Wakatipu (6L–7M), the country's longest lake, and presided over by the jagged peaks of the Remarkables (7M). From here, total immersion in the wilderness of the national parks of Fiordland (1M–2K) to the west and Mount Aspiring (2–3K) to the north is within half a day's drive. The region includes many of the country's most famous tracks—Milford, Routeburn, Hollyford, Greenstone-Caples, Rees-Dart—and you can follow ancient Maori trails through fjord-etched valleys. Be prepared to book the more popular trails, such as the Milford and Routeburn tracks, at least six months in advance

MATAKAURI LODGE, QUEENSTOWN *(7M)*
Lakeside Lair, p. 18

Queenstown can quickly feel suburban and overcommercialized, but just a few miles away, Matakauri Lodge (2L) takes you far away from that. You can be as gregarious or low-key as you like here, and do as much or as little as you want. The property's private beach is nearby, as is Bob's Cove (6M), one of the most scenic spots along the Queenstown–Glenorchy Road. The food is fantastic; Gerhard Gerber, one of the country's leading chefs, prepares a daily menu with an emphasis on Central Otago ingredients—salmon, Bluff oysters, and venison—and local wines. But the views of the ripple-free lake are the reason to come.

CONTACT: Matakauri Lodge, Glenorchy Road, Queenstown, tel. 03/441–1008, fax 03/441–2180, www.matakauri.co.nz. 4 cottages, 3 suites.

DISTANCES: 5 mi (8 km) from Queenstown, on the road to Glenorchy (2L).

PRICES: NZ$534–NZ$872 double per person; NZ$802–NZ$1,308 single occupancy. Rates include before-dinner cocktail hour with canapés, three-course dinner, full breakfast, local telephone calls and connections, transfer on arrival and departure, and GST.

OPTIONS: If you visit **Arrowtown** (7M) and any of the nearby vineyards, don't miss a lunch or dinner at **Saffron** (18 Buckingham St., Arrowtown, tel. 03/442–0131) and a stop at **Chard Farm** (off Hwy. 6, Gibbston, tel. 03/442–6110; open daily 10–5), close to the Kawarau Bridge bungee-jumping site (7M). For pure drama, it's hard to beat a helicopter ride, which offers an overview of this spectacular region—from Queenstown to Fiordland and along the glaciated West Coast—so much of it otherwise inaccessible. **Queenstown Heliworks** (Queenstown International Airport, Tex Smith Lane, Box 2211, Queenstown 9197, tel. 03/441–4011, fax 03/441–4012, www.heliworks.co.nz) starts at NZ$1,880 for a 1-hr ride for 4 people.

VENTURING FORTH IN QUEENSTOWN (2L)
A Shot of Adrenaline, p. 56

Queenstown is an enormous, open-air adventure playground. You can go white-water rafting, jet-boating, twin parapenting (like paragliding, but with a parachute-like device), canyoning (like rappelling), river boarding—where do you want to start? Several locations offer bungee-jumping (Queenstown is where the sport was commercially launched, in 1988). Some of the companies that guide walkers along the region's famous tracks are based here, too. In winter, between June and October, the main adrenaline-pumping sports are skiing and snowboarding, at the local areas of Coronet Peak (7M) and the Remarkables.

CONTACT: Everything you could possibly want to know about or book, including bungee jumping and the Shotover Jet, is available at the Station Information Center (Shotover St. at Camp St., Queenstown, tel. 03/442–5252, www.thestation.co.nz).

AJ Hackett, Queenstown (The Station, Box 488, Queenstown, tel. 03/442–7122 or 0800/286–495, www. ajhackett.com). Shuttles for the **Shotover Jet** (Box 189, Queenstown, tel. 03/442–7087 or 0800/7468–6837, www. shotoverjet.co.nz) leave from the station. Queenstown Visitor Center, (tel. 03/442–4100, qvc@xtra.co.nz). Queenstown Information Center, (tel. 03/442–7319, info@queenstowninfo. co.nz). For more information about booking guided walks, check out www.ultimatehikes.co.nz. A good general Web site is www.queenstown-nz.co.nz.

PRICES: Bungee jumps at Kawarau Bridge start at NZ$125; Shotover rides start at NZ$79.

OPTIONS: Steep yourself in the glorious landscape outside Queenstown, near Arrowtown, at the **Loose Box Guesthouse** (730 Hwy. 6, Lake Hayes, tel./fax 03/442–1802, www.the loosebox.com; NZ$610 double, including breakfast and GST), a stylish lodge converted from an historic building that originally served as a stable, wool shed, and loft. Rooms include Santa Fe touches alongside Georgian antiques. The self-contained guest wing has an open-plan kitchen and sitting room. **White Shadows Country Inn** (58 Hunter Road, Queenstown, tel. 03/442–0871, fax 03/442–0872, www.white shadows.co.nz; NZ$495, including breakfast and GST) has magnificent mountain views across nearby Coronet Peak. Its schist stone cottage, separate from the main homestead, has two suites, each with a stone fireplace, wood-beam ceilings, and glass-roof bathrooms that look out at beech trees and landscaped gardens.

TAKING TO THE SADDLE IN GLENORCHY (2L)
Riding the High Country, p. 52

From Queenstown, the meandering stretch of road that follows the west arm of Lake Wakatipu to the pioneer village of Glenorchy ranks among the loveliest in the country. Bordered by two national parks—Mount Aspiring and Fiordland National Park—it is the gateway to a wilderness of rugged high country perfect for a horseback outing. If an afternoon isn't long enough, you can opt to spend several days in the saddle, trekking the backcountry and sleeping in rustic cabins in the nearby hamlet of Paradise (6L). Glenorchy goes completely horse mad during the **Glenorchy Races,** held the first Saturday in January. To soak up the local atmosphere and gossip, drop into the charmingly recherché **Glenorchy Café;** on the main street, it's a favorite of film-maker Jane Campion, who lives nearby.

CONTACT: Groups led by **Dart Stables** (contact Peter Davies, Box 47, Glenorchy, tel. 03/442–5688, 0800/743–464, fax 03/442–6045, www.glenorchy.co.nz) never have more than 5 riders; all skill levels are accommodated. Helmets, oilskins, and refreshments are provided, but be sure to wear comfortable trousers and shoes and warm layers and bring sunscreen.

DISTANCES: Glenorchy is 25 miles (48 km) from Queenstown.

PRICES: NZ$65 for a 2-hr ride; NZ$130 for 5–6 hrs; and NZ$300 for an overnight trek or NZ$700 for a 3-day, 2-night trek, including all meals, accommodation, and GST.

OPTIONS: Dart River Jetboat Safaris (Mull Street, Glenorchy, tel. 03/442–9992, 0800/327–8538, fax 03/442–9075, www.dartriverjet.co.nz) operates jet-boat safaris up Dart River (6L) that provide close-up views of ancient beech forests, glaciers, and waterfalls. In terms of lodging, Glenorchy offers nothing much in between backpacker's palaces and **Blanket Bay** (Box 35, Glenorchy, tel. 03/442–9442, fax 03/442–9441, www.blanketbay.com; NZ$1,190 doubles–NZ$1,790 suites), which overlooks the north end of Lake Wakatipu and the frosted Humboldt Range (6L–N). The palatial retreat, on a 65,000-acre sheep station, has 13 sumptuous rooms (7 of them suites) and a friendly, attentive staff of 20; it feels like a decadent cross between a Bhutanese palace, a Sun Valley hunting lodge, and a California spa. It's hard to imagine a more congenial place to return to after a day of horse-trekking, fly-fishing, hiking, or flightseeing. Rates are for 2 people and include use of all sports facilities, breakfast, before-dinner drinks, and dinner; GST is not included.

FIORDLAND NATIONAL PARK (1M-2K)
Into the Sound, p. 32

Carved out by huge ice-age glaciers, Fiordland is New Zealand's largest national park and one of the wettest places on the planet. Its 3 million acres include precipitous granite mountains, long narrow fjords, steep valleys, deep lakes, dense forests, wild rivers, transient waterfalls, and some of the most remote coastline imaginable. Milford Sound (5L) is the region's best-known destination, mostly for the breath-catching sight of Mitre Peak (5L) looming nearby; you reach it either by walking the Milford Track (5L–M), which begins near Te Anau Downs (5M), or by driving along Milford Road. The views, of flowery fields, roadside waterfalls, mossy forest tracks, draw your attention almost constantly. At the entrance to Homer Tunnel, which leads you down the last hill toward the sound, playful green kea—alpine parrots—peck and pounce on people's cars, nibbling at windshield wipers. Another good way to explore Fiordland is by boat. Whatever you do, be sure to bring strong insect repellent and wet-weather gear.

CONTACT: Rosco's Milford Sound Sea Kayaks (Box 19, Milford Sound, tel. 03/249–7695, www.kayakmilford.co.nz) offers guided kayaking on and around Milford Sound from NZ$49 per person. You can go on half- or full-day guided walks through ancient beech forest in Fiordland, part way on a section of the Milford Track, or join a day tour (NZ$115) that includes a cruise on Milford Sound with **Trips and Tramps** (Box 81, Te Anau, tel. 03/249–7081, fax 03/249–7089, trips@teanau.co.nz).

DISTANCES: Milford Sound is 75 miles (120 km) northwest of Te Anau (2L), 180 miles (290 km) west of Queenstown.

OPTIONS: From Milford Sound, **Fiordland Travel** (Box 94, Queenstown, tel. 03/442–7500 or 0800/656–503, fax 03/442–7504, www.fiordlandtravel.co.nz) runs day cruises on the *Milford Monarch* and the *Milford Haven* and overnight cruises on the *Milford Wanderer* or the more luxurious *Milford Mariner*. Aboard the *Mariner,* which has private cabins and en suite bathrooms, NZ$250 per person covers a shared cabin, all meals, GST, and kayaking. The *Fiordland Navigator* leaves Manipouri (2M) for overnight cruises into Doubtful Sound (1L); NZ$340 per person covers a shared twin cabin, all meals, and GST, with kayaking and a ride in a glass-bottom boat. You can explore Doubtful Sound and farther afield into Fiordland National Park, even as far as Stewart Island and New Zealand's Sub Antarctic Islands, aboard the **Breaksea Girl** (tel. 03/249–6600 or 0800/ 249–660, fax 03/249–6600, www.sp.net.nz/eco.htm), a 125-meter (413-ft.) steel ketch based in Doubtful Sound. Owners– skippers Lance and Ruth Shaw, committed conservationists, offer a variety of natural-history and ecotourism experiences, including 3- to 10- day cruises and guided sea kayaking. *Breaksea Girl* operates year round, can accommodate up to 12 people, and has central heating for those nippy Fiordland nights. Rates are NZ$195 per person, including GST; chartering the boat costs NZ$1,950.

QUEENSTOWN AND FIORDLAND HIGHLIGHTS

In town, take in the lakeside and mountain views from the **Queenstown Gardens** and nurse a swirled cappuccino in one of the many cafés. The **Skyline Gondola** ferries you up Bob's Peak, 1,425 ft above the lake, for the ultimate postcard views. Minutes from Queenstown is the 1860-era gold-mining settlement of Arrowtown, with modest, Victorian-era cottages and a valley setting. It's at its most resplendent in autumn, when the surrounding hillsides of beech trees turn russet, helping to create a soft carpet underfoot. This entire region is also great driving country, and it's worth finding time to explore the dramatic backcountry of **Skipper's Canyon** (7L) and at least see **Kawarau Bridge,** even if you have no plans to make any leaps. Neighboring **Central Otago,** with its former gold-mining settlements, lakes, and vineyards, is becoming known for its pinot noir.

New York-based photographer Simon Russell spends most of his time chasing his 5-year-old son, Aidan, with a camera, trying to get a picture of the perfect moment—thousands of shots later. In the quiet moments he lounges in the garden with his wife, Ann, sipping fruity New Zealand wines—a wonderful new habit. Photo assignments in the Big Apple keep him busy most of the time. However, for a little excitement, he travels the world seeking out wonderful places to photograph. His work has been published in *National Geographic, Trips, Blue, Condé Nast Traveler,* and other periodicals worldwide. *Escape to New Zealand* is his third in the *Fodor's Escapes* series (following Morocco and Ireland). The adventures he had all over Aotearoa (Land of the Long White Cloud), as the Maori call it, were a dream assignment.

Author Kirsten Ellis, a New Zealand native based in New York City, was delighted to return to the country she left when she was 17. She has worked in Hong Kong and India for the *South China Morning Post,* with assignments ranging from investigating India's supermarket of ashrams to camel-trekking in the Thar desert, and has written six travel books, on India, Cuba, the Philippines, and the Maldives. A Fellow of the Royal Geographical Society, she has also written for *The Australian, New Zealand Herald, World Eye Reports, Tatler, Discovery,* and *The Explorer's Journal.*